# Immigrants and Religion
## in Urban America

How shall we sing the
Lord's song
in a foreign land?
If I forget you, O
Jerusalem,
let my right hand wither!
Let my tongue cleave to the
roof of my mouth,
if I do not remember
you,
if I do not set Jerusalem
above my highest joy!

*Psalms* 137: 4–6

# Immigrants
# and Religion
# in Urban America

*Edited by*
*Randall M. Miller and Thomas D. Marzik*

Temple University Press
Philadelphia

Temple University Press, Philadelphia 19122
© 1977 by Temple University. All rights reserved
Published 1977
Printed in the United States of America

International Standard Book Number: 0-87722-093-X
Library of Congress Catalog Card Number: 76-062866

# Contents

# Preface

This collection of essays, reflective of the latest research in immigration history, grew out of a series of symposia entitled "Religious Freedom: Churches and Ethnic Communities in the American City" which was held at Saint Joseph's College, Philadelphia, during the academic year 1975–1976. An urban, multi-ethnic institution, the college sponsored the symposia in order to celebrate the American Bicentennial and its own one hundred twenty-fifth anniversary. The integrating theme of the symposia was the relationship between religion or religious beliefs and the ethnic experience in post–Civil War urban America. The essays included in this volume were selected on the basis of their compatibility with that theme. All the authors have revised or rewritten their papers after their oral presentation.

Whether explicit or implicit, the essays have an urban setting, and save for Dennis Clark's chapter on the Irish and Jay Dolan's chapter on the Germans, all treat the "New Immigration" of the late nineteenth and early twentieth centuries. Historians have learned that all cities were not alike, and they are beginning to understand that all immigrant experiences were not alike. Before the full history of immigration and cultural pluralism in America can be written, each immigrant group in each geographic setting must be studied intensively. The essays in this book, which focus on several Eastern and Midwestern urban communities, suggest the wide range of contrasting experiences within and between immigrant groups in different urban settings.

In discussing the role that religion played in defining and preserving ethnic character and helping the immigrants to adjust to conditions in urban America, the authors have used the term religion broadly. It includes both the formal institutions of religion such as churches, schools, and social organizations, and the intangible belief systems and customs—folkways if you will—of the immigrants. It also includes religious figures who interacted with the immigrants as preachers, teachers, labor leaders, and social workers.

Finally, the authors examine immigrant religion at its vitals—in the parish, the congregation, the school, the sweatshop, the home. This book is about the immigrant people as much as it is about their religious institutions and faith. More than bricks and mortar of new synagogues or parish schools, more than Sabbath preaching, religion was the lifeblood of the immigrant communities. It was the vehicle for national aspiration, the purveyor of good counsel on labor disputes, education, and family, and the timetable for the life cycles of birth, growth, and death. Religion provided continuity to the immigrants. It bridged the Old World and the New World and made adjustment possible and bearable. The essays in this book explore the meaning of the formal and informal religion of various immigrant groups and tell us why their religious expression endured.

In a project of this scope there are many debts—too many to recount and honor here. We hope that the brief mentions below will be some small recompense for the cooperation and support this project and book have received from so many people and institutions.

The idea for the symposia—the seed for the book—largely originated from discussions with James Gallagher and Eve Brunswick in 1974, both of whom laid the groundwork for the symposia. From the beginning Thomas P. Melady, the college's executive vice-president, provided unflagging, enthusiastic encouragement and mobilized the full resources of the college to promote the program and the book. His vision and commitment to ethnic studies was a source of constant inspiration. Daniel N. DeLucca and Mary Lou Finlayson joined the project in 1975 and made it their own. Ably assisted by Christina Abendroth, Patricia Casper, and Stephanie McKeller, they worked tirelessly to bring the series to fruition. Dan and Mary Lou handled the myriad details of funding and administration with skill and tact. More than this, they transformed the symposia into a major bicentennial celebration of ethnic life in Philadelphia, and by bringing local religious and ethnic leaders and laymen to the campus to share in the program, they helped to bridge the gap which often separates scholars from the public. In many ways this is as much their book as it is ours.

Throughout the series the project received the very active encouragement of Howard L. Applegate, Philip F. Mooney, and the staff of the Balch Institute as well as cooperation from numerous local ethnic organizations. Individuals who played significant roles in the series of symposia either as participants or supporters were: the Reverend Zaven Arzoumanian, George J. Beichl, James M. Bergquist, the Reverend David J. Bowman, Phyllis Pease Chock, Eileen Z. Cohen, Sebastiano DiBlasi, Reinhard R. Doerries, John B. Duff, the Reverend John J. Falatek, Murray Friedman, Francis C. Ganiszewski, Frank X. Gerrity, Louis L. Gerson, Caroline Golab, Theodore Hershberg, Lawrence N. Jones, Richard N. Juliani, Joanna Karvonides, Edward Kolyszko, Bertram W. Korn, Eleanor E. Krkoska, Myron B. Kuropas, Zenon Kwit, Gregory G. Lagakos, Joseph Monte, Michael Novak, Joseph P. O'Grady, Bohdan P. Procko, Lawrence D. Reddick, Theodore Saloutos, Herta M. Stephenson, Peter G. Stercho, James H. Tashjian, James H. J. Tate, the Reverend Terence Toland, Constantine Tsirpanlis, Robert Ulle, Richard A. Varbero, and Constance L. Williams. To all of them we extend our thanks.

This book has profited immensely from the careful readings it received from several readers and from Kenneth Arnold, Michael Ames, and the staff at Temple University Press. John M. Mulder read portions of the manuscript and made numerous valuable suggestions for improving style, organization, and argument. Philip Mooney also contributed insightful and useful criticism. Richard Juliani had several suggestive observations to offer when the book was in its formative stages. Any success this book enjoys owes partly to their friendly yet rigorous criticism. Since we did not always heed their counsel, we can hardly hold them account-able for any errors.

Finally, special thanks are due to the patrons and sponsors of the ethnic symposia. They provided financial assistance which helped to underwrite the series and to bring this book to print. The project received generous contributions from the following patrons: C. Thomas Gibbons of Horn and Hardart Baking Com-pany, the Goethe Institute, Thomas F. Hayes of the Philadelphia Gear Corporation, John B. McClatchy, Dennis J. J. McGee of McGee and Company, and Joseph J. McLaughlin of the Bene-ficial Savings Bank. Others who sponsored the project with fi-nancial support were: the Honorable Francis A. Biunno, Leo Draus, John R. Durkin, Louis J. Esposito, Mr. and Mrs. John R. Finlayson, Mr. and Mrs. Francis C. Ganiszewski, the Reverend Francis A. Gwiazda, Joseph P. Kowacic, Mr. and Mrs. Charles P. Krkoska, John S. Sabatino, the Honorable and Mrs. Albert F. Sabo. We hope that this book will justify their confidence and their unselfish devotion to free intellectual inquiry.

R. M. M.

# Introduction

## Randall M. Miller

America is an immigrant nation. Although this statement is so apparent that it is almost a truism, it remains largely misunderstood. For most Americans, the facts of immigration seem scarcely worth additional attention. Many Americans believe that the process of assimilation somehow reshaped the various ethnic and religious groups from Europe to produce a common American character. The process was perhaps painful for some, particularly the so-called "New Immigrants" from Southern and Eastern Europe who came in the late nineteenth and early twentieth centuries. But the process was necessary and real, and it occurred at a relatively rapid rate. By the second generation assimilation was completed. The children of the European immigrants grew up as Americans far removed from the cultural, linguistic, and religious world of their parents. Or so the story goes.

The long history that this assimilationist interpretation of the American immigration experience has enjoyed reveals America's deeply felt need to define an American character. The environmentalist logic of the eighteenth century, the nation's formative period, maintained that American forests and republican virtue would cleanse European immigrants of Old World contaminants. Hector St. John de Crèvecœur said it best in his *Letters from an American Farmer* (1782) when he described the American as a "new man," an individual transformed into a distinct social type. In a large, diverse land with untested institutions, Americans derived a certain comfort from the notion that somehow they would all turn out alike and that everyone would share the American dream. The consensus of American politics reflected a supposed consensus of American culture. Throughout the nineteenth century, in their histories, their literature, and their speeches, American writers and public men echoed the assurance that Providential design and American republicanism would continue to do the good work of transforming Old World men into new Americans. That often astute and eloquent social commentator, Alexis de Tocqueville, wholly embraced this theme of assimilation as the handmaid of frontier democracy and gave it a persuasive permanence in his influential *Democracy in America* (1835). With that, the assimilationist model entered the American lexicon.

The floodtide of European immigration in the late nineteenth century, of strange new peoples from strange new lands, challenged this confidence. So too did the dislocations of urbanization and industrialization. The "New Immigrants" entered an America that was rapidly urbanizing and industrializing. The pace of life everywhere quickened. Mules gave way to tractors on the farms, and carriages gave way to streetcars in the cities. Improvements in communications, transportation, and the distribution of goods broke down rural isolationism and accentuated rural-urban differences. It was an America that worshiped rugged individualism but produced trusts and urban political machines. It was an America of strident nationalism which disguised national self-doubt. It was an America of progress and poverty. In many ways, the immigrants' future, as indeed America's future, depended on their ability to adapt to the new industrial, urban order—to make sense out of this land of paradox.

But the appeal of the regenerative power of the American environment and republican institutions continued to offer the promise that even the unwashed, unlettered hordes from Southern and Eastern Europe would learn American ways, honor American traditions, and so prosper. It would take time and effort, of course, and there was a growing number of doubters among nativist Americans, but the myth of assimilation endured

and adjusted to meet the new crisis. Indeed, it received its most
graphic expression in Israel Zangwill's 1908 play, *The Melting
Pot,* which cast America as a great crucible "melting and refin-
ing" the races of Europe into a new alloy of Americanism.

The melting pot analogy, however, has always had an unap-
pealing rigidity about it, for it implies that the mold of American
character and institutions was formed with the republic—that
newcomers had nothing really fresh or useful to contribute to the
American character. For a nation that celebrates change, this was
an unsettling proposition. Thus even the most distinguished advocates of assimilation have revealed an ambivalence toward the
crucible metaphor. Furthermore, as John Higham has recently
written, the melting pot is a sinister "industrial image, fraught
with the menacing heat and the flashing intensity of a steel mill,"
which contrasts sharply with the eighteenth and nineteenth
century pastoral ideal of the purifying properties of the virgin
land. By taking the assimilation process out of the forests and
fields and putting it in the factory—the new focus of American
promise and the real "home" of the immigrants—the proponents
of one America conceded that rigorous new methods were
needed to remold the "New Immigrants." Their old habits were
too ingrained and too foreign for easy cleansing, and there were
too many of these strange people arriving in America to rely on
the older, more gradual process. Progress and the integrity of
American institutions demanded a speedy metamorphosis among
the immigrants lest they transplant the corruption and decadence
of the Old World in the New.

This shift from the pastoral to the industrial metaphor points up
the failure of the assimilationist interpretation to explain ade-
quately the immigrant experience in America. Differences, after
all, exist and persist, and few immigrants willingly divested
themselves of their past. The immigrants were not passive
recipients of "American" culture. They came to America with
cherished institutions and values, and many came as members of
cohesive communities capable of resisting Americanizing
pressures. In fact, their responses to American conditions con-
tinually fed the evolution of American culture. The rhetoric of
assimilation has often obscured or ignored these countervailing
trends in American immigration history. Conflict as much as

consensus has marked the American experience. As the essays in this book make clear, ethnic and religious rivalries between immigrants and nativist Americans and between immigrants and other immigrants are the stuff of American immigration, indeed of American history.

The evidence for diversity in American life is compelling. From the anti-Irish riots of 1844 through the immigration restriction movements of the twentieth century, nativist Americans have reacted strongly against the tenacity of Old World cultures and imposed powerful demands on immigrants to conform to New World mores. Immigrants, in turn, resisted pressures to conform as best they could. The responses varied according to time and place, circumstances, and the peculiar culture of each immigrant group. Itinerant workers from Southern and Eastern Europe, for example, had little inclination to learn anything but the most rudimentary American ways, for they had little interest in settling permanently in America. In contrast, Armenian Protestants escaping the ravages of hunger and oppressive government in the Old World and partially acculturated by virtue of their conversion to Protestantism at the hands of American missionaries necessarily made concessions to American culture in exchange for jobs and acceptance in American religious and social institutions. Many of the "New Immigrants" huddled together in reconstructed villages—the "ghettoes" in the industrial cities—where they carried on Old World social, religious, and familial customs. In their families and in their religions they sought comfort and relief from employers and those who would have them give up their identity as Czechs, Poles, Germans, Jews, Irish, or whatever, The Irish worshiped in Irish parishes, drank Irish whiskey, and elected Irishmen to municipal offices. Germans read German papers, listened to German sermons and music, drank German beer, and voted for German politicians. The "New Immigrants" attempted to repeat the process of self-promotion with equal zeal. Poles married Poles, Italians married Italians, and so on. More than this, the transplanted peasants sought out others from their home villages or, failing that, from their native region. Rather than disintegrating, the structure and content of life of the Old World flourished in the New.

This is not to say that being Polish-American, Italian-

American, Irish-American, or German-American was the same thing as being Polish, Italian, Irish, or German. Indeed, they were very much different. In the intense heat of pressures to conform and to learn the clock-time rhythms of the industrial working world, some melting surely occurred, more for some than for others. Not all immigrants were well insulated. But in varying degrees a distinct ethnic consciousness and identity survived for each immigrant.

If the immigrants did not wholly slough off their Old World customs and folkways, they hardly divorced themselves from their religion. Carrying their beliefs with them to America, the immigrants attempted to recreate their communal life of the Old World by implanting their traditional religion in America. They initially sought to do this by participating in the American religious institutions which most closely resembled their own, or they imported their religious establishment wholesale.

But the immigrants' religion transcended their reconstruction of the ritual and institutional forms of the Old World faith. Religion was intertwined and imbedded in the psyche, the folklife, the very identity of each immigrant. It gave meaning, a system of moral values, self-definition, and community to the immigrants. It ordered their internal, private world and the world outside the family. Thrown into close proximity with competing cultural and linguistic groups in industrial, urban America, the immigrants turned to religion, the very bone and sinew of ethnicity, to shore up communal ties. With family and job, religion was the focal point of immigrant life. The form and function of the various expressions of the immigrants' religions is the subject of this book.

At its most visible level, organized religion provided immigrants with a rich institutional life which introduced them to the complexities of a highly organized, industrial world. Organized religion performed many useful functions. It rendered educational, social, material, and spiritual services, and in a crude way helped to settle the immigrants in America. In the absence of public social services, individual priests, pastors, and rabbis interceded on the immigrants' behalf to find them jobs, food and shelter, and acceptance. Many immigrants sustained themselves during hard times on the charity and humanity of concerned clergymen. In addition, a few sympathetic clergymen invoked the church militant to wage war against oppressive employers, landlords, and public officials.

The religious establishments were the only institutions to which the immigrants had access that wielded power in America. But it was a reluctant power, grudgingly given. Acts of charity and support for the immigrants' many political, economic, and social needs were generally individual acts of individual clergymen. No major religious group in America after the Civil War had a reformist hierarchy committed to ameliorating the lot of the poor, the laboring, and the alien. Within each religious group a variety of nationality groups contested for power against other nationality groups. By and large, the Irish dominated American Catholicism, German Jews controlled American Judaism, and native-born Americans of Anglo-Saxon heritage directed the affairs of American Protestantism. All were advocates of assimilation and cooperation with the American political, economic, and social establishment. The price for their assistance in the immigrants' struggle to survive and prosper in urban America was conformity. It was a dear price.

As this book illustrates, the religious institutions became battlegrounds of ethnicity and nationalism. Unable to control them, some disgruntled immigrants broke away to form their own; others retreated to their homes and jobs; others accommodated themselves to the demands of the religious leaders. The struggles within the religious establishments pushed many clergymen, however slowly, closer to accepting a concept of cultural pluralism and promoting the interest of their polyglot adherents, but not before losing the trust and loyalty of many immigrants and their children.

American Catholicism is a case in point. It has long been a staple of American Catholic Church history, popularized by Will Herberg among others, that the Church scored remarkably well in helping the Catholic immigrants to adjust to American conditions, and in the process broke down national and cultural barriers separating the various ethnic groups. The Church was the crucible in which Irish, Germans, Poles, Italians, Czechs, Slovaks, and others were melted down and mixed to become the American Catholic amalgam. Supposedly, the Catholic immigrants emerged with a common Catholicism and conservative social outlook, and the Church supposedly retained the loyalty of legions of Catholic immigrants. At the same time, the Irish bishops and priests, who had gained control of the Church machinery by the 1850s, instructed the later arrivals in American political and civic ways and taught them to revere American institutions, through a "green" lens of course.

But as the chapters on Catholic immigrants show, many Southern and Eastern European Catholics arrived in America with a deep-seated distrust of formal religious institutions, especially the Church hierarchy, and the very respectability and ties of the Irish prelates to the American establishment made the American Catholic Church hierarchy suspect in the immigrants' eyes. Where the Irish built churches and supported priests, the *contadini* looked upon priests as parasites and preferred to live their faith out of doors in the *festa* and indoors in their family devotions and magic. The *contadini* remembered the Catholic Church as a landlord in Southern Italy exacting high rents, as a temporal power retarding Italian unification, and with its army of Northern Italian priests as an interloper bleeding the Southern peasants. Similarly, the Polish peasants, although intensely loyal to Catholicism and much less hostile to the priesthood than were the *contadini,* also regarded the Church hierarchy warily. In the partitioned Poland of the nineteenth century the episcopacy sometimes obstructed nationalist drives and took an indifferent or condescending attitude toward the Poles.

Southern Italians, Poles, even Czechs and Slovaks in varying degrees, brought their suspicions of the Church hierarchy to America. Here they confronted an American Catholic establishment overwhelmingly dominated by the Irish. For the Irish, Catholicism had become the great fortress of national preservation in Ireland. In America the Irish won control of the Church bureaucracy and used the Church's resources to further the economic, political, and social ambitions of their countrymen. The Irish hierarchy argued for assimilation and recoiled from the "pagan" and casual religious practices of the Catholic immigrants from Southern and Eastern Europe. The clashes between the Irish and the Germans and later between the Irish and other immigrant groups form the leitmotif for many of the chapters in this book. The clashes revealed the resiliency of ethnicity among the immigrant groups, the fantastic proliferation of religious beliefs and practices of the different Catholic immigrants, and the politics of assimilation in American Catholicism.

The clashes occurred at many levels, but most intensely at the local level—in the parish, on the job, in the schools, wherever men and women of different nationalities congregated. The clashes reverberated throughout American Catholicism and eventually led to the establishment of national parishes. Through their schools, their newspapers, and their churches, all conducted at least partly in their native languages, the Germans and then the Southern and Eastern European immigrants fought off both the Protestant and Irish-American Catholic brands of Americanization, with mixed success.

What happened in Catholicism also occurred to a lesser degree in American Judaism and Protestantism. The religious diversity of America, a heritage from the colonial period, multiplied enormously in the late nineteenth and early twentieth centuries. It challenged what Martin Marty has described as the "Righteous Empire" of Anglo-Saxon Protestant cultural and religious hegemony. It tested America's religious tolerance and the elasticity of the American religious establishments. The profusion of new religious expressions brought by the immigrants and the intensity of the immigrants' attachment to their traditional religious identities transformed the American crucible into the American mosaic. Although the authors disagree on the success of the Americanizing process which occurred in the American churches, they do agree that it did not eradicate ethnic identity. For better or worse, it redefined it.

The eight chapters in this book explore the complexities and dimensions of the immigrants' religious beliefs and practices and how religion and religious leaders shaped the immigrants' attitudes toward America, work, family, and self. They suggest important variations in the patterns of belief and adjustment to America among different groups of immigrants, and they further illustrate how different immigrant groups interacted with one another. Finally, by treating non-Protestant groups, they remind us that American history and the American religious heritage do

not derive solely from Protestant and Anglo-Saxon origins. The
slow, gradual, and painful recognition of the dimensions of religious and cultural pluralism in modern America emerged from
the interaction between Protestants and non-Protestants and
between the various non-Protestant groups themselves. In-
somuch as these essays recover that past, they demonstrate the
need to face the implications of pluralism in religion and society.

   Josef Barton and Rudolph Vecoli concentrate on the internal
religion of Czech and Southern Italian immigrants respectively.
They provide detailed descriptions of the folk religion and community life which prevailed for each group in the Old World in
order to understand the process and product of the attempts by
Czech and Southern Italian immigrants to reconstruct their religious and communal lives in America. For both Czechs and
Southern Italians religion was local and family oriented, and it
strengthened the continuity of life between the two continents of
their residence. Kinship ties of the extended family, reinforced as
they were by a common folk religion of feast days, patron saints,
and for the *contadini,* magic, determined the associational life of
the immigrants in America.

   The formal associational, institutional life of the immigrants
and the struggles for national identity within the Catholic Church
are two of the underlying themes of the next four chapters. Although the American Catholic Church pressed in upon the "New
Immigrants" to conform to established religious and social
norms, the presence of competing immigrant groups in the
Church threatened to shatter Catholic unity. Still, the Church
provided opportunities for leadership for each group, and friendly
priests sheltered their various countrymen from some of the
worst abuses of an alien, hostile world. And as the essays suggest, however indirectly, the American Catholic Church proved
to be a malleable institution capable of embracing differing
cultural groups and religious lifestyles.

   Dennis Clark argues that the revitalized Catholic Church of
mid-nineteenth-century Ireland helped to inform and to inspire
increased Irish activity in the Church in America. Confronted
with a dynamic, but often inhospitable urban environment in
America, the Irish moved into the Church bureaucracy in the
American cities in order to fulfill their social needs. This

experience peculiarly fitted them for success in modern, corporate America by teaching them managerial skills in the complex
Church hierarchy. They learned to wield power. In a very real
sense, the Irish made over the American Catholic Church into a
training school and social welfare agency as the Church made
over the simple Irish peasant folk into the principal defenders of
the American Catholic Church, modern city dwellers, and
resourceful, independent managers.

Jay Dolan's chapter on the German Catholics in Philadelphia
discusses some of the implications of the Irish dominance of the
American Catholic Church. To meet the challenges of Irish
Americanizers, German Catholics devised strategies of resistance
and accommodation which partially preserved their ethnic
identity. They constructed their own hospitals and asylums,
printed their own newspapers, ran their own schools and cultural
organizations, and lobbied for separate national parishes in the
American Catholic Church.

Control of education was crucial to ethnic survival. William
Galush continues this theme in his chapter on Polish immigrant
religious education and associational life. The bitter contests
between Irish and Polish leaders over the issue of the national
parish often focused on the specific question of direction of parochial school instruction. Although the Poles gained some control
over their own schools and priests, they were losing the struggle
to maintain a distinct ethnic culture within an Irish-dominated
church. Time ran against them as it did against the Germans.
Their children increasingly adopted American habits of speech
and social custom, left their neighborhoods for jobs, lost interest
in the native language and culture, and married outside the group.
Polish identity survived, but in a diluted form.

Contrariwise, Mark Stolarik finds that Slovak priests, who remembered with horror the baneful effects of Magyarization in the
old country, successfully erected barriers to assimilation by opposing formal education of Slovak children beyond the primary
grades. Slovak priests rejected the so-called "Protestant ethic"
of material ambition, diligence, and sacrifice, and they communi-
cated these sentiments to their parishioners in America. Slovaks
prized continuity and stability rather than rapid economic and

social mobility and so better avoided the compromises of culture necessary for economic success and advancement in America.

The final two chapters treat interethnic and intra-ethnic rivalries of two non-Catholic immigrant groups. Maxwell Whiteman points out the consequences of the different concepts of Judaism and different cultural values which separated the established, affluent German Jews from the incoming tide of poor East European Jews. In Philadelphia the work requirements of the garment industry disrupted the religious lives of the East European Jews who were employed there. Moreover, German Jews exploited religion by appealing to the common Jewish heritage to forestall Jewish garment workers from organizing against them. Indicative of the sensitive role of religious leaders, and of the limitations of such men in satisfying all the conflicting interests of their flock, Whiteman describes the role of Rabbi Sabato Morais, shuttling back and forth between German Jewish employers, trade unionists, and East European Jewish garment workers, in trying to reach a settlement of a protracted labor dispute in the Philadelphia garment industry.

Religious leaders and intragroup conflict also figure prominently in Robert Mirak's chapter on Armenian immigrants. Mirak contrasts the history of assimilation of Armenian Orthodox and Armenian Protestant immigrants. The Armenian Orthodox church leaders enforced the old religion in America and resisted encroachments on culture and belief. The isolation of their religion from the American religious mainstream helped to insulate their community. Armenian Protestants, however, more rapidly adjusted to American life, despite the sometimes hostile reactions of nativist Protestants. Immigration was a selective process, as revealed in the propensity of converted Armenian Protestants to emigrate. They were already a people apart in the Old World as a consequence of their new faith, and they sought prosperity and acceptance among fellow Protestants in the New World. As with all the immigrants discussed in this book, the Armenians, both Orthodox and Protestant, sacrificed and struggled to recreate their religious lives in America. This was powerful testimony to the depth of their beliefs and the centrality of religion in their everyday lives.

The great American historian, Frederick Jackson Turner, once wrote that to understand America it is necessary to understand the immigrants. This book extends that equation by suggesting that to understand the immigrants it is necessary to understand their religions. Together, the eight chapters constitute a preliminary reconnaissance into the history of the immigrants' religions, a subject too long ignored. From different perspectives all the authors remind us of the vitality and force of religion as a factor in defining and preserving ethnic life and character in America.

# Immigrants and Religion
# in Urban America

Chapter 1

# Religion and Cultural Change in Czech Immigrant Communities, 1850–1920

Josef J. Barton

Of all the dimensions of that ambiguous process of transformation
that we call immigration—at once a sign of change and an agent of
change—surely the most difficult to grasp is the religious. Not
often does one find dramatic upheavals, or critical elections, or
frightful propaganda. Convenient measures of change and continuity certainly do not exist. We learn something about the social
context of religion when we talk about the sweep of urbanization,
or the emergence of class solidarities, or the movement toward
occupational specialization; but such talk tells us little about the
meanings and forms of religion itself. In the life of a religious
community, old wine flows as easily into new wineskins as new
into old. This presents an elusive problem, for often it is difficult
not only to say just how the shapes of religious experience are
changing but whether they are changing at all. Worse, it is not
even clear just what things one ought to look for in order to find
out.

The temptation is to offer a definition of religion, then to
characterize the probable relationships between different forms
of social life and varieties of religious expression. From succumb-
ing to this temptation come those tiresome discussions of the role
of religion which sound like an argument between the village
atheist and the village preacher—or among their more sophisti-

3

cated equivalents, those trolls with large vocabularies who must punish their listeners with phrases like "functional" or "dysfunctional," "ego strengthening" or "anxiety producing," and so on. The question with which we begin is simple, although hard to answer: just what sorts of beliefs and practices support what sorts of faith under what sorts of conditions? If we ask this question, the overall questions about the strengths and weaknesses of religion disappear like the phantoms they are, and we are left with the task of completing particular evaluations, assessments, and diagnoses. "Our problem," Clifford Geertz remarked recently, "and it grows worse by the day, is not to define religion but to find it."[1]

We will not find it in a burning bush or in the good earth; rather, we must look for religion's sustaining symbolic forms and social usages. Immigration, whatever else it involved, meant an astonishing journey from one cultural and social world to another. As an individual decision and as a mass movement, immigration violated one of the cardinal requirements for community of any sort, namely the need for continuity, for stability of orientation—in a word, for identity. In just those contexts where men and women act—the religious, the political, the familial, and the personal—immigration produced radical change. How, then, are we to understand the symbols and metaphors which newcomers used to characterize social reality? And how are we to find the ways in which institutions made these images and metaphors available to those needful of them?[2]

Clearly, we want to look for the particular and the concrete, hoping to find in the little what eludes us in the grand. But a difficulty lies here in the thick accretion of conventional observations upon the surface of immigrants' experiences. The story of immigration, when told in epic dimensions, often partakes of myth, and the clichés of which myths are made freeze whatever fluency our inquiries might have. The religious past of a newly created immigrant community becomes a convention, and the image becomes a static vision. At this point, as Walter Ong observed some years ago, "the American Catholic comes face to face with a difficulty of his own. It is from somewhere in this past that the Faith has come." With this series of stroboscopically frozen poses, continuity must be preserved; yet he discovers himself "committed as a Catholic to a past whose static qualities his own American situation has exaggerated for him." Tradition-directed when he set out from his village, the Catholic immigrant characteristically learned to take his cues from a new American context without a violent interior wrenching. The adaptation seems now so commonplace, so much taken for granted, that no one bothers to explain it.[3] This adaptation, this creation of a mass urban religious culture, has become the screen through which we see reality and the mirror we hold up to our past.[4]

Bootless, then, is another attempt at definition. What we need are real boots in order to follow men and women from the time they left their villages to the time their children started their own households. Patterns of immigration selected particular people and led them to settle in particular locales. The choices of immigrant leaders and the development of local associations shaped the life of the new community. Rearing children, learning to labor in an industrial economy, and watching their sons and daughters leave the household and form their own families—these events, too, reveal the diverse meanings which urban life held for the immigrants. Religion shaped these actions, then, when men and women, as a result of shared experiences, felt and articulated the identity of their community in images of pilgrimage, carnival, labyrinth; and when those symbols became available in ritual and institution. We need, then, to watch these men and women over an adequate period of change, for a religious community is defined as its members live their own history. So, as Lucien Febvre remarked, we should have one preoccupation in these matters—to understand and to understand from within.[5]

In order to gain a view from within, what we need is not the distracting illusion of generalization, but particular observations, notes from another country. Happily, when we speak of Czechs, there are available none of those viral phrases which plague the study of other American groups. I am thinking, for instance, of "Irish authoritarianism," or the "Italian mother complex," and so forth. We can start out fresh to produce the long-term and fine-comb research which can give palpable actuality and sensible reality to a story. The sort of material used here—the collective biography of Czech priests, the description of a first communion in a Chicago parish, the narrative of a religious festival in a mining town—is best gathered in small settings. This is good strategy not because a parish is the world in a few blocks. What one finds in a parish is parish life. But these small facts speak to large issues, or at least, when coaxed into a comparative setting, they can be made to do so.[6]

Emigration was a symptom of important changes in the peasant villages of Eastern Europe, and it also hastened change. Peasants left a world on the wane, a society in disaggregation. The development of national markets for agricultural products and the transformation of land, especially communal pasturage and forests, into just another commodity threatened the order of the village and the status of peasants. These changes left the peasantry in perpetual ferment, but without the cohesion to give collective expression to its aspirations and needs. So when faced with hardship, a large proportion of small landholders chose emigration as an alternative to the old order.[7]

The areas of heaviest emigration in Eastern Europe—southern Bohemia and Moravia, eastern Slovakia, Galicia, Transylvania— were characterized by a relatively broad distribution of property and mixed agricultural systems. The redistribution of property and the development of commercial agriculture had gone far enough to create a countryside in which large and small holdings, all labor intensive, were ranged side-by-side. A few large proprietors formed the upper stratum of the social structure, while a second stratum of middling cultivators enjoyed some expansion as alienated estates and communal lands passed into the hands of a rural petite bourgeoisie. An even larger group of small owner-operators who produced enough for their own households and a tiny surplus for the towns occupied a third stratum. Finally, a sizable group of laborers made up the largest segment of the agricultural labor force.[8] Traditional agricultural practices and relatively broadly distributed property muted inequalities of income. Hence emigration affected most strongly those regions where agricultural development was most backward, and where an equality of misery characterized the society.

The distinctive characteristic of the regions of heavy emigration, then, was a diffusion of property rights which ordinarily provided households and dowries for sons and daughters of peasants. By no means was this an egalitarian society; rather, traditional agriculture and relatively broadly distributed property reduced inequalities of income. The practice of partible inheritance continued to fragment land and to provide at least a scrap of land for new generations. It was such miserable patrimonies which tied men and women to their villages. The broad distribution of property rights, the use of sharefarming and sharecropping, the growth of communal credit agencies—all these factors supported a peasant agriculture. Emigration was symptomatic, then, not of some general crisis in peasant agriculture, but of the growing imbalance between the needs of peasant households and the opportunities for nonagricultural employment. What had contributed to the stability of peasant households before the 1880s was the close connection between agriculture and household industry. But everywhere the spurt of agricultural modernization (and hence of specialization) and the decline of household industry (because of the penetration of manufactured goods into the countryside) restricted the peasants' resources. Unable to find a piece of land in already crowded villages, young men and women who once would have become apprentices and artisans abandoned the land altogether. And as their chances of finding work in the village narrowed, they joined a world market of labor.[9]

The crowded railroad cars arriving at Bremerhaven and Hamburg carried Czech villagers, not members of an abstract nation. That mirage of utopia was still the possession of bourgeois nationalists. It was through the village that peasants were integrated into agrarian society, that laborers found daily employment, and that artisans disposed of their wares. The inhabitants of these villages belonged to part-cultures in continuous interaction with the outside world. Small-holding peasants of the Moravian village of Huslenky depended upon seasonal migration during the nineteenth century for the little cash they needed to buy new tools or land. By the 1870s, young men began to venture to Brno (Brünn) for construction work, to Ostrava for a season in the textile mills, finally to St. Louis and Chicago. By 1890, every peasant household of the village had sent a member to some Czech or American city in search of work.[10] From Polná, a small village near Havlíčkův Brod, a steady stream of young men and women flowed first to farming areas of Wisconsin, then to the industrial shops of Cleveland and Chicago.[11] After 1870, a characteristic restlessness appeared among the inhabitants of a great variety of villages, a seasonal movement first, then a search for employment in local industries, finally a journey toward an European or American city. Few households escaped the effects of this mobility. All villages experienced the changes wrought by this rural exodus.[12]

But more than an unsettling restlessness, this mobility was symptomatic of a felt loss of mastery in the villages. The cycle of communal ceremony, the liturgical procession of the year, now less satisfied the need for order. In presenting the occasion for enacting family relations at baptisms, weddings, funerals, namedays, and the commemoration of patron saints, ritual practice performed for all to see the single largest fact of village social structure: the very large measure of autonomy and self-reliance of the nuclear family. Other ritual occasions, such as Christmas, Holy Week, and "Greetings" to Mary, bolstered the shared identity of families as members of a community. In these discrete performances of ritual, Czech Catholic villagers encapsulated the world as lived and the world as imagined. Here, in these little observances of the year, peasants attained their faith as they portrayed it.[13] Sunrise, noonday, sunset; spring, summer, autumn, winter: the world as peasants lived it met the world proclaimed in liturgy, to fuse in a plastic drama.[14] So the enormous variety of family and communal feasts flowed with the diastole and systole of the year, marking both the imagined events of salvation and the real events of social interaction.[15] Ceremonial focused, then, on behavior, on a set of rules which rendered action predictable and assured social order.

The erosion of the household economy and the astonishing mobility of villagers after 1870 slowly weakened the web of familial and communal affiliations. Festival and ritual depended upon the active participation of all present, upon the breaking of boundaries between spectators and actors. Time ceased to be succession and became another time, situated in a mythic past. The festival was a dream of how wonderful it would be if times were always good. Dreams make a difference, at least so long as they express a real pattern of social life.[16] A pilgrimage to an old shrine, circumambulation of a parish together with family and neighbors, the dedication of a saint's statue—all these events enacted the relationships among individuals and groups in the village. An incongruity appeared, however, between the cultural framework of meaning and the patterning of social interaction. The cycle of communal ceremony expressed real participation in communal life. When that participation diminished, as Jan Neruda discerned in a visit to a textile village in 1866, a sense of dissonance entered the life of the community.[17]

The disaggregation of community life came slowly, sometimes imperceptibly, everywhere accompanied by a dissolution of the communal economy and its rhythms. And nothing was more emblematic of this decadence than the peasants' and laborers' loss of common lands. The slow but steady usurpation of pasture and forest by a new village bourgeoisie shut off access hectare by hectare, until by the 1860s the communal economy was dead.[18] The resonance of this transformation was felt in every area of peasant society, but most acutely in the household. The rhythms of work, once intermingled with social life, became synchronized with the demands of commercial agriculture and wage labor. On estates and in villages, growing numbers of peasants were drawn into some sort of organized wage labor after 1870. Family life was governed less now by collective rhythms and more by an impersonal labor market.[19]

In this new situation, in which families lived exposed to the vicissitudes of an external economy, peasant families adopted two strategies of defense. First, they developed a network of kinship ties outside the household, ties which were important resources of aid and economic activity. In Moravian Huslenky these ties bound families through dowry and donation, through apprenticeship and foster parentage, through mutual aid. There emerged, then, a cohesive and overlapping structure of small groups, an informal collective life in which kinship linked a number of households.[20]

Secondly, families formed voluntary associations to create organizations which gave collective response to their new vulnerability. Hence there emerged an enormous variety of associations in the 1870s and 1880s to insure against illness and death, to supervise education, to form trade and agricultural schools, and to pursue political aims. In Huslenky, a village of about twelve hundred inhabitants, at least fifteen associations flourished between 1870 and 1890. Masons formed a mutual benefit society, share tenants an agricultural society, tinkers a burial union. In Polná, a similar array of associations developed after mid-century. Several agricultural societies, a mutual-aid society of hand-loom weavers, and a burial society of carpenters assured residents membership in one or another association.[21] The cumulation of economic and social changes in the villages fragmented households into many groups, each concerned to secure its position by creating new coalitions. Voluntary associations furnished a means of achieving an appearance of stability in a changing world.[22]

Within this context of fragmentation and partial integration there emerged a new religious life. The festival, the old instrument of articulating the collective rhythms of cultural and social life, remained the vehicle of religious activity. But important changes occurred in village ceremonial, the first of which was a proliferation of private festivals among allied family groups. Often enacted on the nameday of the oldest among a group of brothers, these little observances expressed the interdependence of households. And more, family festivals created a widening circle of contacts for children, a rhythmic intimacy which marked all the important events of young lives. Here was a new pattern, another weaving, of human living, of whose fabric each individual became a part. Not even death frayed this figure, for the visit to the cemetery became the continuing religious act of a family in the mid-nineteenth century and remains so today.[23]

More apparent than this mutation of sociability was the emergence of an enormous variety of religious associations. Feast days, shrines, patron saints—these now required associations in order to maintain an increasingly fragmented religious observance. Occasionally the older collective rhythms would break through, during the harvest in a Czech village or during lambing time in a Moravian hamlet. But the various traditional features of village religious life now only indirectly expressed the growing differentiation of households and of groups to which they belonged. Where once the ritual life of a Bohemian village had for a moment effaced social boundaries in an enactment of communal solidarity, now each performance brought together only a segment of the community.[24] By the end of the nineteenth century, peasant families had achieved a partial yet enduring cohesion of household and community in which religious associations and ceremonies played the largest part. Within these crosscutting ties, individuals and families clung to a tangible communal identity.[25] After all other impressions fade, this one remains— together with that of the loss of any felt cohesion in the community, save that which peasants, in response to a profound transformation of labor and social relations, built for themselves.

The mass emigration began in the time of troubles between the disaggregation of the communal economy and the consolidation of a new agrarian regime.[26] First to feel out of place in their own land were artisans, who often became pioneers of migration streams which emptied whole villages of their inhabitants. Once a settlement was established in Cleveland or Pittsburgh or Chicago, a community took shape. The pattern of migration itself—the predominance of migrants from a few villages or a few districts— assured that most of the newcomers would encounter familiar faces, dialects, and social customs. Arrivals from well-represented homeland districts early established demographic and social hegemonies in settlements, partly because of sheer numbers, but also because they tended to annex, through marriage or other means, large numbers of the immigrants from sparsely represented regions. Traditional loyalties to village and neighborhood took hold in a favorable demographic context during the lifetime of the first generation and shaped the communities' cultural lives.[27]

The emergence of immigrant communities was in part a reconstitution of old models of order and in part an accommodation to the life of the city. Newcomers looked backward, to a village past, as well as forward, to an urban future. Already familiar with the use of voluntary associations in community life, immigrants set about constructing a "tangible organizational reality" within which newcomers could identify themselves and declare their solidarity with a people.[28] But since Czech immigrants were drawn from hundreds of villages, the urban communities were no mere transplants of the old villages. Rather, they were made up of specialized associations meeting partially the needs which peasant households and the villages of which they had been a part had fulfilled comprehensively. It was in this accommodation that immigrants developed distinctive orientations toward the problems and prospects of the city.[29]

The cities, especially those burgeoning giants on the bleak flat land of the Midwest, assumed after 1870 the new patterns of the industrial metropolis. Chicago, Pittsburgh, Cleveland, and Detroit all counted a growing proportion of their inhabitants foreign-born after 1880. Work patterns changed also, for what had been cities of laborers and merchants in 1880 had become filled with clerical and sales workers by 1950. The motley sources of population growth and the diversification of occupational structure created new social arrangements, the most important of which was residential segregation of ethnic, racial, and occupational groups. The laggard response of public institutions to urban problems meant that private institutions were extremely important. The family, the neighborhood, the voluntary association became the principal agencies of social control and reform between 1890 and 1950. These characteristics, then, defined the new world of Czech immigrants and structured the course of their lives.[30]

However unfriendly the modern city appears, the passage from village to metropolis was no sudden plunge into modernity. The very fragmentation of urban life created interstices in which local communities could create and sustain a humanly satisfying culture. It was here, in these discontinuous circles of urban life and work, that immigrants learned to live in the city. And in so doing, they traced a pattern which defines our own urban religious inheritance.[31]

This patrimony was a weave of small patterns, an outcome of thousands of decisions made in household and workplace. Crucial to an understanding of urban religious culture is that it was the possession of agricultural laborers, peasants, and artisans— newcomers who took half a lifetime to learn to be industrial laborers, owners of city lots, and skilled machinists.[32] The members of cultural elites in immigrant communities ordinarily came from an intellectual petite bourgeoisie who had even in the village put off any remnants of peasant culture. This tiny group of newspaper editors, bankers, and merchants were busy tagging behind their urban counterparts, eager to cash in on a fashionable nationalism. In the Czech community, their chance would not come until the 1920s.[33] Working-class immigrants inherited the aging core of the cities, and there they built for themselves a distinctive culture. Mike Gold puts the case bluntly in *Jews without Money:* "[The city] was my world; it was my mother's world, too. We had to live in it, and learn what it chose to teach us."[34]

The fact that the bulk of Czech immigrants began their lives as unskilled laborers is a decisive one in interpreting their experiences, for their beginning at the bottom of the occupational hierarchy meant that most families would not escape manual labor. But newcomers did not remain in identical class positions. Even though mobility was largely within the working class, the movement of unskilled laborers into skilled jobs or their purchase of property represented significant gains over their origins.

Family mobility, as recent work on American cities between 1880 and 1960 shows, fell into three crude patterns.[35] I have learned in the middle of a study of 360 Czech families in Chicago that slightly less than a fourth of unskilled newcomers and their sons remained laborers for the whole of their lives. Both the immigrants and the second generation took jobs as hod carriers or furnace stokers. Their wages left them little margin, and their employment provided few opportunities to acquire skills. Nevertheless, many men who had begun as laborers managed to gain skills and property. A little less than 60 percent of the families of Czech laborers in my Chicago sample eventually moved into the skilled and propertied segment of the working class. In about half of this group, family members acquired skills, while in the other half families advanced their fortunes through the purchase of property.

The workshops of this remarkable achievement were the subdivided homes of DeKoven Street and the tenements of Eighteenth Street.[36] Biographies convey this experience better than a sociological filter of finest mesh. František and Marie Sládek came to Chicago from Zahrádka, in Bohemia, in 1874. They had three children—Anton, born before they left Europe, and James and Frank, both born in Chicago—none of whom attended school beyond the fifth grade. František worked as a laborer in a railroad yard, earning between $360 and $480 a year;

Anton, the oldest son, began work in a planing mill at sixteen, earning about $250, while James became a tailor's apprentice at twelve, working twelve hours a day for two dollars a week. When they pooled their earnings, it was enough to buy a tiny house on Twelfth Street and to set aside ten dollars a year in a savings account. Life was crowded but satisfying in this house, where all the sons lived into their thirties.

Look at the themes in the lives of another ordinary family. Václav Jerášek came to Chicago from Polánka, in Moravia, in 1877. He married Barbara Lišková from neighboring Hovězí, and together they had two daughters. A laborer in a brick yard, Václav earned $560 in 1880, most of which went for family expenses except for twenty dollars which he deposited in a building and loan society. This account grew slowly, but amounted in 1890 to a down payment on a seven room house on Canal Street, which Václav and his wife shared with Maria and Anna and their husbands for twenty years.

The need for roots, the search for stability and continuity is reflected in these family histories. As the constitution of a Czech Catholic workers' society had it, Christian family life depended on "diligence in duty, attendance at Mass, Catholic schooling, and frugality."[37] The story of Josef Hlavatý and his family, from Budišov, illustrates these themes. Josef and Kateřina arrived in Chicago in 1881 with two children. They found a tiny apartment in a tenement occupied by ten Czech families. Josef finally found work as a construction laborer, while Kate took in washing. Josef, the oldest child, was apprenticed to a boiler maker at age thirteen in 1886, became a master of his trade in 1893, and set up his own shop in 1895. Rebecca went into service at fourteen, married a Polish ticket agent, and became head of an enormous household of her own children and her husband's relatives.

Family life in such households took the form of connected networks of social relationships, first to relatives and secondly to friends. Immigrant families lived within overlapping connections of kinship, of neighborhood, of association. Husband and wife brought to marriage an already closely knit network of ties. The birth of children, which brought godparents into the family, created new connections. Each family member, each relative, became a link not only with other kin but with people outside the family as well. Across the open frontiers between households flowed relatives, boarders, mutual assistance. In these tangential circles of intimacy flourished a dense, but informal, collective life.[38]

A remarkable growth of voluntary associations accompanied the emergence of immigrant family life. Czech newcomers to Chicago formed forty-nine mutual benefit societies between 1870 and 1880, thirty-one of which began as branches of societies in homeland villages. Each society drew families and neighborhoods into wider circles of mutual aid and set off a process of association which eventually pulled most families into a round of organized life. Choirs and theater groups performed daily in the new halls and saloons, self-improvement societies offered workers literacy and polish, bakers' and butchers' and framemakers' societies bound together men of a trade, while the members of the Eagle Bicycle Club terrorized plodding pedestrians along Blue Island Avenue. Wherever one looks in these new communities, whether along DeKoven Street in Chicago or West 25th in Cleveland, an extraordinary density of associational life meets the eye.[39] In these urban settlements voluntary associations became the characteristic social unit which "provided a matrix within which the group organized its policing devices, family life, marriage, churches, educational system, and associations for cultural and social ends."[40]

Family and community served, not as refuges from the invasion of the world, but as centers of unbounded interaction, the focal points of a crowded social life. Around the family spread a network of relations, increasingly loosely knit toward the periphery. Ceremonial marked most of the events of family relationships. These little acts of sanction, in turn, made of reciprocity a religious as well as familial value. But more importantly, the ritual events surrounding a christening or a first communion marked the entrance of a group of families into symbolic as well as actual interdependence. The year of Czech families in Chicago and Cleveland and St. Louis was punctuated with regular enactments of the varied events of family life. Each observance brought renewed awareness of the fellowship to which they belonged. The first communion of fifty-nine children at St. Procopius, Cleveland, in 1880, began at nine in the morning with a little parade along a sidewalk lined with parents and neighbors and ended, after a day filled with celebration and carnival, in a huge feast.[41] Community life began with these occasions, in which family members bound themselves to each other in enactments of Catholic life. A gathering of the heads of young families on West 25th in Cleveland marked the emergence of parish life; a meeting of seventeen young men in Milwaukee in 1880 led to a new Catholic youth organization; an assembly of older women in Chicago produced a sodality for the aged.[42] Families who were natives of the same village, or belonged to a widening circle of relations, or remembered feasts once enjoyed in the homeland, found each other in these new associations. Each association provided the needed relationships for which a periodic gathering of families was a metaphor. Each symbolic enactment shaped expectations of family order.[43]

Ties which bound also divided. The essential feature of religious associations in new communities was their multiplicity, in which was expressed the fragmented character of community life. The astonishing proliferation of saint's societies, each a mutual benefit organization as well, filled the calendars of urban parishes. For a week, a street became an urban village, filled with families from Budišov or Polná. To march around the parish, to keep a midnight vigil at a saint's statue, to hear a panegyric upon St. Wenceslaus, all meant a moment of restoration of another world. The multiplication of saint's societies, of confraternities, of young men's and women's sodalities made of Czech parish life a round of donations and festivals.[44] Every week was marked with the observance of some feast day, every street the scene of a brief pilgrimage through a saint's precinct.[45]

It was in communal feasts, parades, and anniversaries that the larger religious community was affirmed. In these greatly crowded days an older collective rhythm, of which families and neighborhoods were still a part, broke through the newer urban life. In 1884, at the first anniversary of the Czech Roman Catholic Benevolent Union of Chicago, eighteen associations joined in a parade through the streets of Czech settlements. A dramatic club presented several plays on the streets, each on a theme of particular religious significance. On Sunday, after a week of celebration, a great feast was followed by a dance into late Monday morning.[46] These were days of procession, when the whole community was drawn into a representation of solidarity. The newer round of urban work and living ceased for a while as an event in the year's passing was marked. It was here, in just such recurrent dramas, that the religious world of the village and the changeful reality of the city became one. Now became available the metaphors which sustained continuity and identity in familial and communal life.[47]

Within this matrix of relationships emerged that characteristic American activity of parish building. Families, gathered into voluntary associations, lent their energies to the construction of churches, schools, and orphanages, those standard features of urban Catholicism. Beginning with St. John Nepomuk in St. Louis, in 1854, and ending in the 1920s and 1930s in Cicero and Parma and Huntington Woods, Czech Catholics participated in the formation of an urban Catholic establishment. Yet a lively growth of voluntary associations in parishes continued to mediate this participation and to furnish the medium which nourished the exfoliation of Czech Catholicism in the New World.[48]

If my argument has been convincing so far, it should suggest that Czech Catholicism in particular, and urban Catholicism in general, can be understood only over the long run. Czech emigrants left a changing homeland in which peasant families had created new styles of community life. In coming to terms with the unsettling transformations of village life, families had acquired a communal sense, a capacity to respond to collective needs. As Czech newcomers entered the modern American city, they were prepared to seek ways of pursuing their collective needs. The Catholicism to which they gave shape fulfilled the immigrant's urgent need to reach beyond his immediate family for aid and support. This religious life, which found expression in an astonishing variety of festivals, associations, and institutions, both formed the urban Catholicism to which today's Catholics are all heirs and mirrored immigrants' responses to the American metropolis.

Let me pursue this discussion a bit further and suggest some of the ways in which this perspective helps to understand the emergence of urban Catholicism. The Czech pioneers of the first and second generation built institutions which were particularly responsive to the changeful reality of the city. In the first thirty

years of the twentieth century, it was just these new communities
which were most exposed to the corrosive force of urban mobility. Hence immigrant parishes could not freeze in their
development, as happened to urban Protestant parishes, those
mute pickets which now march down Cleveland's Euclid Avenue
or through Chicago's North Side. In Chicago, for instance, the
rapid dispersion of the original Czech settlements and the
development of satellite communities in more than twenty
suburbs created a new need for parish life. Already in 1908 a
Czech priest in an urban parish complained that of 160 families in
his parish, 140 lived more than five miles from the church. And so
the exodus went, until by 1910 the creative center of the Czech
community lay among the bungalows and double-deckers surrounding the Western Electric plants in Chicago's western
suburbs.[49] Here, amidst the new world of efficiency experts and
suburban developers, took shape a Catholicism whose task
was to find some middle way between the opposing perils of self-
isolation and total absorption.[50]

One of the responses of Czech parishes was to form new organizations in order to reach alliances with other Catholic communities. The National Alliance of Czech Catholics, for instance,
grew out of a wartime association into a major representation of
emergent middle-class immigrants. It had a large role in introduc-
ing to second and third-generation Czech families the varieties of
Catholic action groups in the 1920s and served as an avenue
through which a maturing ethnic community participated in a
broadening religious community.[51] The development of such
groups characterized the life of every Catholic ethnic community
in the 1920s. As Czech organizations strove to keep pace with
their changing clientele, then, they took their cues from the
contemporary world. This was bound to provoke a crisis of confidence, for in the same measure that Czech Catholics participated
in this modernization, just so they admitted that their group no
longer had anything distinctive to bring to the larger culture of
Catholicism.

And so began that periodic assimilation and rebuilding which
characterizes modern urban Catholicism. The Americanization of
ethnic Catholicism had just about run its course in the 1950s,
when there began in urban and suburban parishes a reconstruc-

tion of ethnic identities. We do not know very much about this rebirth of Catholic ethnicity, but I think a few guesses might be helpful. In the first place, much of the leadership in the reconstruction of ethnic communities came from men and women who rediscovered, in their own family and community life, the need to reach beyond the household in order to pursue collective goals. Like their grandparents, they recovered a sense of the possibilities of communal life. And again, like their grandparents, in doing so they began to come to terms with the realities of American urban life. In the second place, this committed core of Czech ethnic leaders reached out to an ambivalent or downright suspicious periphery in hopes of strengthening the nucleus of ethnic life. This was not done out of a sense that a Czech ethnic community like that of Chicago in the 1890s can be recreated, but from a drive to raise the quality of that committed core of ethnic leadership. Ironically, in order to achieve this aim, Czech leaders have had to reach across ethnic boundaries for alliances with many other groups. And so, in the very act of gaining new support for the life of the ethnic community, its leaders have discovered what binds together a pluralistic culture. In American life, then, the contrary impulses of separateness and integration continue to work, their implications for the Catholic community still unfolding.

## Notes

1. Clifford Geertz, *Islam Observed: Religious Development in Morocco and Indonesia* (New Haven, 1968), p. 1; see also Geertz, *The Interpretation of Cultures* (New York, 1973), pp. 123–125.

2. Robert N. Bellah, *Beyond Belief: Essays on Religion in a Post-Traditional World* (New York, 1970), pp. 66–67 and pp. 147–148.

3. Walter J. Ong, *Frontiers in American Catholicism* (New York, 1957), pp. 5 and 45.

4. On this point see Robert Warshow, *The Immediate Experience* (New York, 1970), pp. 38–39.

5. Lucien Febvre, *Au coeur religieux du XVIe siècle* (Paris, 1957), p. 334; cf. E. P. Thompson, *The Making of the English Working Class* (New York, 1963), p. 11.

6. I am indebted to Gabriel Le Bras, *Études de sociologie religieuse,* 2 vols. (Paris, 1955–1956), 1: 356–391; 2: 463–481; and to desultory read-

ing in the recent work of French historians of religion, a convenient guide to which is Franco Rizzi, "Storia religiosa in Francia: problemi e tendenze," *Quaderni storici,* 22 (1973), 238–247.

7. Kamil Krofta, *Dějiny selského stavu,* 2nd ed. (Prague, 1949), pp. 407–418 and 423–440; Christoph Stolzl, *Die Ära Bach in Böhmen: Sozialgeschichtliche Studien zum Neuabsolutismus, 1849–1859* (Munich, 1971), pp. 29–40; Ludmila Kárníková, *Vývoj obyvatelstva v českých zemích, 1754–1914* (Prague, 1965), pp. 133–135 and 210–213.

8. Rudolf Franěk, *Některé problémy sociálního postavení rolnictva v Čechách na konci 19. a počátkem 20. století* (Prague, 1967), pass.; Oldřiška Kodedová, *Postavení zemědělského proletariátu v Čechách koncem 19. století* (Prague, 1967), pp. 10–13.

9. Bedřich Šindelář, "Kořeny a povaha českého vystěhovalectví za kapitalismu," in Josef Polišenský, ed., *Začiatky českej a slovenskej emigrácie do USA* (Bratislava, 1970), pp. 13–48; Vladimír Srb and Milan Kučera, "Vývoj obyvatelstva v českých zemích v XIX. století," in František Egermayer, ed., *Statistika a demografie* (Prague, 1959), pp. 122–123 and 146–147. Emilio Sereni develops this argument brilliantly in the context of nineteenth-century rural society in *Il capitalismo nelle campagne (1860–1900),* 2nd ed. (Milan, 1968), pp. 38–39 and 351–369.

10. Field notes, Huslenky, Sept. 1972; Chicago and St. Louis, 1974.

11. Jaroslava Hoffmannová, *Vystěhovalectví z Polné do Severní Ameriky ve druhé polovině XIX. století* (Havlíčkův Brod, 1969), pass.

12. Kárníková, *Vývoj obyvatelstva v českých zemích,* pp. 265–279.

13. Cf. Fred Gearing's work on Greek Orthodoxy, "Preliminary Notes on Ritual in Village Greece," in J. G. Peristiany, ed., *Contributions to Mediterranean Sociology* (Paris, 1968), pp. 65–72, and Geertz, *Interpretation of Cultures,* pp. 112–114 and 163–169.

14. Thomas Merton, *Seasons of Celebration* (New York, 1965), pp. 45 and 49–53.

15. The work of nineteenth-century ethnographers is a good approach to the character of village religious life; see, for example, the summary of this work in Kamil Krofta, *Naše staré legendy a začátky našeho duchovního života* (Prague, 1947). I have found helpful, too, the work of writers like Jan Neruda and Božena Němcová. See especially Němcová's notes on a Czech village in the 1840s, "Obrazy z okolí domažlického," in *Národopisné a cestopisné obrázky z Čech* (Prague, 1951), pp. 9–23.

16. Octavio Paz, *El laberinto de la soledad,* 2nd ed. (Mexico City, 1959), pp. 37 and 39–41.

17. Jan Neruda, *Menší cesty* (Prague, 1961), pp. 199–204; cf. Lumír Dokoupil, "Teritoriální a sociální mobilita populace ostravské průmyslové oblasti v období její geneze a počátečního rozvoje," *Čes-*

*koslovenský časopis historický,* 21 (1973), 355–368. Maurice Agulhon's *La République au village* (Paris, 1970), pp. 147–187 and 207–245, is a fascinating and suggestive account of a similar transformation of a Provençal village.

18. Jaroslav Purš, *Dělnické hnutí v českých zemích, 1849–1867* (Prague, 1961), pp. 42–47.

19. Ladislav Kmoníček, "Námezdní práce na zlonickém velkostatku před a po roce 1848," *Sborník archivních prací,* 7 (1957), 64–78; Gustav Hofman, "Blatenský velkostatek v polovině 19. století," *Sborník archivních prací,* 8 (1958), 124–127; František Kutnar, "Sociální otázka tkalcovská v polovině XIX. století," *Sborník historický,* 2 (1954), 207–217.

20. Field notes, Huslenky, Sept. 1972; Chicago and St. Louis, 1974.

21. Ibid.; Hoffmannová, *Vystěhovalectví z Polné,* pp. 10–20.

22. Cf. Michael Anderson, "The Study of Family Structure," in E. A. Wrigley, ed., *Nineteenth-Century Society: Essays in the Use of Quantitative Methods in the Study of Social Data* (Cambridge, 1972), pp. 49–52.

23. Field notes, Cleveland, Apr. 1968; Chicago and Detroit, 1974; cf. Philippe Ariès, "La Mort inversée," *Archives européennes de sociologie,* 8 (1967), 181–182, and *Western Attitudes toward Death: From the Middle Ages to the Present* (Baltimore, 1974), pp. 65 and 72–73.

24. Antonín Robek, *Příspěvky k historicko-etnografické monografii panství Zvoleněves v první polovině devatenáctého století* (Prague, 1966), pp. 75–81 and 102–103; Hoffmannová, *Vystěhovalectví z Polné,* pp. 10–20.

25. Czech and Slovak historians have not begun to explore this transformation, even though the sources are available; see, for instance, *První valný sjezd katolíků mocnářství rakouského roku 1877* (Prague, 1877), pp. 210–219; František Kryštůfek, *Dějiny církve katolické ve státech rakousko-uherských,* 2 vols. (Prague, 1898–1899), 2: 217–220 and 710–725; *Katolícke Slovensko . . . 833–1933* (Trnava, 1933), pp. 531–538 and 609–619; *Tovaryšstvo,* 1–3 (Ružomberok, 1893–1900). A recent summary shows just how much needs to be done: Friedrich Prinz, "Die böhmischen Länder von 1848 bis 1914," in Karl Bosl, ed., *Handbuch der Geschichte der böhmischen Länder,* 5 vols. (Stuttgart, 1965–    ), 3: 103–123.

Italian historians and anthropologists have begun to publish powerfully suggestive work: Gabriele De Rosa, *Vescovi, popolo e magia nel Sud* (Naples, 1971), pp. 205–239 and 295–317; Pietro Borzomati, *Studi storici sulla Calabria contemporanea* (Chiaravalle, 1972), pp. 171–194; *Aspetti religiosi e storia del movimento cattolico in Calabria (1860–1919)* (Rome, 1967), pp. 63–142; and *I "giovani cattolici" nel Mezzogiorno d'Italia dall'Unita al 1948* (Rome, 1970); Annabella Rossi, *Le feste dei poveri* (Bari, 1969); Clara Gallini, *Il consumo dello sarco* (Bari, 1971). A good report on this work is Antonio Lazzarini, "Studi di storia socio-religiosa," *Quaderni storici*, 26 (1974), 568–581. Zoltán Tóth's work on Romania offers striking insight, especially *Magyarok és románok* (Budapest, 1966), pp. 386–392, and his brilliant study, *Mişcarile ţărăneşti din Munţii Apuşeni pîna la 1848* (Bucharest, 1955).

26. Frank Thistlethwaite, "Migration from Europe Overseas in the Nineteenth and Twentieth Centuries," XIe Congrès International des Sciences Historiques, *Rapports,* 5 (Uppsala, 1960), 50–54.

27. Bedřich Šindelář, "Několik poznámek k otázce našeho vystěhovalectví v epoše kapitalismu," *Sborník prací filosofické fakulty brněnské university, řady historické,* 3 (1954), 18–44; Hoffmannová, *Vystěhovalectví z Polné*, pp. 34–39.

28. Philip Gleason, *The Conservative Reformers: German-American Catholics and the Social Order* (Notre Dame, 1968), p. 10.

29. Family reconstitutions in three Czech parishes in Chicago form the basis of this generalization (N = 360); cf. Josef J. Barton, *Peasants and Strangers: Italians, Rumanians and Slovaks in an American City, 1890–1950* (Cambridge, Mass., 1975), pp. 64–90, where this theme is developed in a comparative perspective.

30. Sam Bass Warner Jr., *Streetcar Suburbs* (Cambridge, Mass., 1962), *The Private City* (Philadelphia, 1968), and "If All the World Were Philadelphia: A Scaffolding for Urban History, 1774–1930," *American Historical Review,* 73 (1968), 26–43.

31. Cf. Timothy L. Smith, "Lay Initiative in the Religious Life of American Immigrants, 1880–1950," in Tamara Hareven, ed., *Anonymous Americans* (Englewood Cliffs, N.J., 1971), pp. 214–249; Sam Bass Warner Jr. and Colin B. Burke, "Cultural Change and the Ghetto," *Journal of Contemporary History,* 4 (1969), 173–187.

32. Cf. Herbert G. Gutman, "Work, Culture, and Society in Industrializing America, 1815–1919," *American Historical Review,* 78 (1973), 540–541, 547–548, 560–563, and 578–580; Marc A. Fried, *The World of the Urban Working Class* (Cambridge, Mass., 1973), pp. 166–169.

33. Author's notes on a study of immigrant leadership in progress.

34. Michael Gold, *Jews without Money* (London, 1930), p. 19.

35. Stephan Thernstrom, *The Other Bostonians: Poverty and Progress in the American Metropolis, 1880–1970* (Cambridge, Mass., 1973); Barton, *Peasants and Strangers.* The following paragraphs depend on some preliminary returns on my reconstitutions of Czech families in Chicago, 1870–1920 (N = 360).

36. See the remarkable report on these areas in City Homes Association, *Tenement Conditions in Chicago* (Chicago, 1901), pp. 21–99 and 184–189.

37. *Čechoslovan* (Chicago), Nov. 20, 1886.

38. Family reconstitutions and field notes, Chicago. I have learned a great deal from Robert Coles's work, especially *Migrants, Sharecroppers, Mountaineers* (Boston, 1971) and *The South Goes North* (Boston, 1971), as well as from the work of British anthropologists: see Elizabeth Bott, *Family and Social Network: Roles, Norms, and External Relationships in Ordinary Urban Families*, 2nd ed. (New York, 1971), pp. 58–60 and 92–95; Michael Young and Peter Willmott, *Family and Kinship in East London* (London, 1957), pp. 81, 91–92, and 134. Michael Anderson's recent study, *Family Structure in Nineteenth-Century Lancashire* (Cambridge, 1971), furnishes a useful perspective in understanding the emergence of urban family life. Australian sociologists have done the best work on immigrant families, to which a good guide is Jerzy Zubrzycki, "The Immigrant Family: Some Sociological Aspects," in Alan Stoller, ed., *New Faces: Immigration and Family Life in Australia* (Melbourne, 1966), pp. 60–74.

39. *Svornost* (Chicago), Jan. 3, 6, 1888; Jan. 14, 18, 31, 1897; *České Chicago* . . . (Chicago, 1900), pp. 13–33; Rudolf Bubeníček, *Dějiny Čechů v Chicagu* (Chicago, 1939), pp. 79–85, 210–217, 295–313, 457–483, and 515–518. Cf. *Pokrok* (Cleveland), Feb. 9, 1875; Jaroslav E. S. Vojan, *Velký New York* (New York, 1908), pp. 40–41 and 48.

40. Oscar Handlin, "The Social System," in Lloyd Rodwin, ed., *The Future Metropolis* (New York, 1961), p. 24.

41. *Hlas* (St. Louis), June 29, 1880.

42. Ibid., Jan. 7, Apr. 28, and Aug. 11, 1880; cf. *Čechoslovan* (Chicago), June 12, 1886; *Věstník* (Cleveland), 1 (Jan. 1, 1903), 5, 14, and 19.

43. See especially the fascinating report of the furnishing of Our Lady of Lourdes, Chicago, by various families of the community, *Národ* (Chicago), Feb. 17, 1895. Cf. *Památník osady sv. Jana Nep* . . . , *1863–1913* (Milwaukee, 1913), pp. 5, 7, 65, and 69; *Památník na zlaté jubileum chrámu Páně Panny Marie Ustavičné Pomoci v New Yorku, 1887–1937* (New York, 1937), pp. 8–30 and 47–53; *Hlas* (St. Louis), Dec. 31, 1879, Mar. 3, 1880, and Apr. 7, 1884.

44. *Pokrok* (Cleveland), Dec. 26, 1874; *Národ* (Chicago), Feb. 7, 14, 1895; *Památník zlatého jubilea osady sv. Václava* . . . *1863–1913* (Chicago, 1913), pp. 37, 43, and 47; *Hlas* (St. Louis), July 28, 1880, Sept. 1, 1880, Oct. 15, 1890; *Volnost* (Cleveland), June 3, 1882; *Album a památník Blahoslavené Panny Marie Lurdské* . . . *1892–1917* (Chicago, 1917), pp. 70–113; *Katolík kalendář* . . . *1905* (Chicago), pp. 170–171; *Památník stříbrného jubilea osady sv. Víta v Chicagu, Ill., 1888–1913* (n.p., n.d.), pp. 57–58; *Hlas kalendář* . . . *1916* (St. Louis), p. 183.

45. See the listing of ceremonies and occasions in one Chicago parish from 1889 to 1897 in *Památník* . . . *sv. Víta,* pp. 19–33, and in *Památník*

*na oslavu stříbrného jubilea osady sv. Ludmily . . . 1891–1916* (Chicago, 1916), pp. 45–59.

46. *Čechoslovan* (Chicago), May 17, 1884; cf. *Hlas* (St. Louis), May 7, 1890; *Památník . . . sv. Ludmily*, pp. 13, 19, and 21.

47. My treatment of these seemingly trivial events owes much to E. P. Thompson, "Time, Work-Discipline, and Industrial Capitalism," *Past and Present*, 38 (1967), 56–97; Dominique Schnapper, *L'Italie rouge et noire* (Paris, 1971), pp. 45–53 and 59–79; William Kornblum, *Blue Collar Community* (Chicago, 1974); Gerald D. Suttles, *The Social Order of the Slum* (Chicago, 1968); and especially to Philippe Ariès, *Centuries of Childhood* (New York, 1962), pp. 395 and 415.

48. *Centennial of St. John Nepomuk Church . . . 1954* (St. Louis, 1954), pp. 40–43 and 65–66; *Zlaté jubileum osady sv. Prokopa, 1874–1924* (Cleveland), n. pag.; *Památník . . . sv. Víta*, pp. 74–77; *Zlaté jubileum osady sv. Víta* (Chicago, 1938), n. pag.; *Památník stříbrného jubilea osady sv. Jana Nepomuckého, 1902–1927* (Cleveland, 1927), n. pag.; *Hlas* (St. Louis), Mar. 30, 1898; *Národ* (Chicago), Feb. 7, 1904; *Památník osady Blahoslav. Panny Marie Lurdské . . . 1908* (Chicago, 1909), p. 9; *Památník oslavy 25-letého trvání osady Blahoslavené Anežky České v Chicagu, Ill.* (Chicago, 1929), pp. 62–66 and 72–114; "Celoroční zpráva osady sv. Víta, 1932," Archives of St. Procopius Abbey, Lisle, Ill., f. "Chicago: St. Vitus."

49. *Zlaté jubileum osady Panny Marie Dobré Rady* (Chicago, 1939), pp. 6–8; *Zájmy lidu* (Chicago), Mar. 28, 1924; Rudolf J. Pšanka, ed., *Zlatá kniha československého Chicaga . . .* (Chicago, 1926), pp. 190–191 and 211.

50. Philip Gleason's essay, "The Crisis of Americanization," in Gleason, ed., *Contemporary Catholicism in the United States* (Notre Dame, 1969), pp. 3–31, is a splendid statement of this dilemma.

51. *Bohemian Review*, 1 (March 1917), 15; *Hlídka* (Chicago), 1 (Aug. 20, 1920), 4–5 and 7; ibid., 1 (Sept. 20, 1920), 1–3 and 5; ibid., 1 (Jan. 1921), 3; *Denní hlasatel* (Chicago), Oct. 12, 1921.

Chapter 2

# Cult and Occult in Italian-American Culture
## The Persistence of a Religious Heritage

Rudolph J. Vecoli

"Pagan! Heathen! Idolator!" These were among the epithets
hurled at the Italian immigrants around the turn of the century. In
addition to being viewed as potential *mafiosi* or anarchists, the
sons of Italy had the further onus of being regarded as the bearers
of anti-Christian beliefs and practices. The "Italian Problem" in
its religious manifestation had been discovered by American
churchmen, both Catholic and Protestant, well before 1900. In
the following decades much energy, money, and ink were
expended in efforts to find solutions to this "problem." What
exactly was the nature of the Italian Problem? With few exceptions, American Protestants *and* Catholics agreed that the Italian
immigrants were characterized by ignorance of Christian doc-
trine, image worship, and superstitious emotionalism. In short,
they were not true Christians.[1]

Given the evangelical zeal of the American denominations,
they quickly defined the Italians as a home mission field in need
of their ministering care. Catholics and Protestants alike established churches, schools, and settlement houses in a competitive struggle to win the Italians for their respective faiths. What
little has been written about the religious life of the Italians in
America tends to deal with various facets of that struggle. There
have been relatively few studies which delineate the actual re-

25

ligious beliefs and devotional practices of this ethnic group.[2]
What in fact was the religious culture of Italian immigrants? And
what has become of this religious heritage among the second and
third generations?

To write the history of the inner life of a people, of its "sacred
cosmos,"[3] is no easy thing, particularly if, like the Italian immigrants, the group has left few personal documents. The historian,
however, can supplement the all-too-scarce letters, diaries, and
autobiographies with the writings of anthropologists, folklor-
ists, sociologists, and churchmen. Drawing upon such diverse
sources, this chapter attempts to delineate the religious culture of
the Italians and its encounter with American Catholicism.

Certainly among the millions of immigrants from Italy, one
could find represented the entire spectrum of religious attitudes:
from devout believer to militant atheist. In late nineteenth
century Italy, positivist and materialist philosophies were gaining
many converts among the educated classes, and increasingly
among artisans and industrial workers. But the immigrants to the
United States tended to be drawn for the most part from the
peasantry of the more isolated regions of Southern Italy.
Southern Italy, the Mezzogiorno, was as yet little affected by the
ideological and technological changes which were transforming
European society. The *contadini* (peasants) of the South, who
comprised the majority of the immigrants to America, continued
to live according to a centuries old way of life. Their folk religion
was a syncretic melding of ancient pagan beliefs, magical
practices, and Christian liturgy. Cult and occult had fused into a
magical-religious world view which was deeply rooted in the
psyche of this people.[4]

The life of the *contadini* was hard, mean, and cruel. The margin
of survival was always paper thin; an illness, a drought, or a dead
mule spelled disaster. Such calamities, however, did not occur at
random; all things found their causes in the malevolent or benevolent workings of the spirit world. For the peasants, religion and
magic merged into an elaborate ensemble of rituals, invocations,
and charms by which they sought to invoke, placate, and thwart
the supernatural. Within their "sacred cosmos," every moment
and every event was infused with religious and magical significance.[5]

In their own eyes, the *contadini,* of course, were *cristiani.* Not to be a Christian was to be an infidel—a Turk. But the peasants' folk religion had little to do with the dogmas or polity of the Church. For such folk, intent upon daily survival, the Christian doctrines of sin, atonement, and salvation had little significance. For the Church as an institution and for its clergy, the peasants felt little affection or reverence. The Church they had known as an oppressive landlord allied with their historic exploiters, the *signori* (upper class, expecially landlords). The priests, often relatives or *paesani* (fellow villagers), they regarded familiarly and even contemptuously. Celibate and dressed in women's garb, the priest was a sexual anomaly in a society which prized virility as the highest male attribute. Yet in the carrying out of their priestly functions, the clergy were respected and even feared. In the popular imagination, the priest was regarded as an archmagician with powers to exorcize evil spirits. The Church played a vital role in the rites of passages, signified by baptism, marriage, and burial, and in the ministration of these sacraments the priest was indispensable. But to those forms of religious observance which were highly prized by American Catholics—regular attendance at Mass, confession, and Holy Communion—the *contadini* were less attentive. While women frequented Church for Mass, novenas, and special devotions, men rarely attended except for the feast of their patron saint and at Easter.[6]

Like all else in the peasant's life, his religion was spatially limited to his particular *paese,* his native village. This spirit of *campanilismo* (excessive village loyalty and parochialism) was expressed in the veneration of local sanctities; each *paese* had its churches and shrines dedicated to its patron saints and madonnas. In religious as in other matters, the *contadini* subscribed to the system of *clientelismo.** God, like the king, was a lofty, distant figure who would hardly have time to listen to the peasant's complaint about his dry cow, but the local saint, as a friend of God, could serve as an intermediary. The cult of the saints thus served as the focus for their formal devotional practices. The saints of Southern Italy were legion: San Rocco,

*Clientelismo* means patronage of saints, more specifically a special devotion to a particular saint who will provide protection or favors.

Santa Lucia, San Michele, San Gennaro, la Madonna del
Carmine, and many others, some whose names "will not be
found in any hagiology." Each saint had special powers to cure a
particular disease, to render a certain favor, or to assure success
in a trade or occupation; one prayed to San Biagio in case of a
throat ache, to Santa Rita for women's ailments, or to San Fran-
cesco di Paolo if one were a fisherman. In their entreaties to the
saints, the faithful were not simply making prayerful appeals;
rather, they regarded these supernatural beings as personalities
who could be enlisted in their cause by the performance of certain
acts. As A. L. Maraspini has observed:

> The saint is not the blessed soul in paradise of orthodox Catholicism,
> who may be venerated, and may, if he so pleases, intercede on behalf of
> his miserably sinful worshipper, but has been reduced almost to the level
> of a familiar demon who can be compelled by a form of words and ac-
> tions to perform certain actions which the operator requires. For the
> peasant does not pray to the saint in the pious hope that the latter may
> take pity on him or that by any meritorious act he may deserve the saint's
> sympathy; he believes that the saying of the prayer, the lighting of the
> candle, and the offering of the ex-voto, are in themselves sufficient to
> enforce the saint's interest on his behalf.[7]

Should the saint fail his petitioner, he stood in danger of having
his statue or image cast out or destroyed in retribution.

The religious life of the *paese* reached its climax with the celebration of the feast day of the patron saint. For the *contadini,* the
*festa* (feast day) provided one of the few releases from the year-
round cycle of work and want. Putting aside austerity for the day,
they indulged themselves in food, drink, and emotions. Dressed
in their festive garb, they packed the church for the High Mass
when the priest delivered the panegyric, declaiming the life and
miracles of the saint. Gifts of money, candles, or grain were
brought to the church in fulfillment of vows made during the year;
sometimes the ex-voto took the form of wax reproductions of
parts of the body which had been miraculously cured. In the
afternoon, the statue of the saint was carried in procession
through the streets, accompanied by the religious confraternities
in colorful robes, a brass band, and the throng of the devotees.
During the procession, emotions reached a high pitch among the
chanting women with wailing, weeping, and trancelike behavior.[8]

The *festa* was also a communal celebration in which all classes and conditions participated. It was a rare opportunity for feasting, dancing, and amusements; animal sales, vendors' booths, and games of chance made it also a country fair. The *festa* ended with a spectacular display of fireworks.

In these festivals, there was keen rivalry among villages and parishes in honoring their respective patrons. Local patriotism as well as religious fervor accounted for the expenditure of "extravagant sums in firecrackers, bands, and illuminations." The administration of the *festa* was in the hands of a lay committee, not of the Church, and contributions for the festival were solicited among the *paese*'s emigrants in America. Their generous response resulted in the increased grandeur of the celebrations. Enclosing a contribution, Angelo di Angelantonio wrote to his sister: "We *americani* have sent this money in order to make a gift to the Very Holy Virgin of Angels because we must do honor for our *paese*."[9] In addition to the sense of vicarious participation, such gifts were made as offerings in return for blessings. The immigrants had no doubt that the Madonna could make miracles in America as well as in the *paese*.

As Ann Cornelisen commented, in the Mezzogiorno there was "a sense of magic in religion" and "a sense of religion in magic."[10] In the peasants' folk religion, the supernatural practices extended far beyond the rites sanctioned by the Church. There were certain areas of the spirit world where the ministrations of the priests were to no avail. No evil befell the *contadino* which could not be attributed to the *mal'occhio* or *jettatura* (evil eye). An erring husband, a sick child, or a poor crop were all caused by malevolent spirits. To counter such curses (or perhaps to cast a spell of one's own), the peasants had an assortment of charms, amulets, potions, and incantations. Each daily act such as the baking of bread or the sowing of grain, had its associated magical formula to ward off evil. When the curse was strong, recourse was had to a *mago* or *strega* (magician or witch), who possessed arcane skills in making and unmaking magic spells.[11]

The folk religion of the *contadini* was no Sunday affair. Rather, it was a total system of beliefs and practices, a "sacred cosmos," in Thomas Luckmann's sense of the domain in which "both the ultimate significance of everyday life and the meaning of extraor-

dinary experiences are located." Judged by the criteria of depth
of conviction and emotional intensity, certainly the piety of the
peasants were real. Their religious faith was not abstract, intellectual, or individual; rather, it was concrete, emotional, and
communal.

Naturally the emigrants carried this religious culture with them
as they went out into the world in search of work and bread.
When they disembarked at Ellis Island, they wore the *corno* (the
coral or gold charm) to protect them against the evil eye.
"Together with the other aspects of southern folklore," Carla
Bianco notes, "the magical-religious world view followed the immigrants to the new shores and stayed with them for several
generations."[12]

The spirit of *campanilismo* was the basic cohesive force which
brought the *paesani* together in neighborhoods and small towns
across America. As soon as a sufficient number of townsmen had
assembled, they formed a society named after the patron saint
and busied themselves with the celebration of the feast day. As
the number of Italian immigrants increased, these societies proliferated by the score and then the hundreds. Statues of the saints
and madonnas, exact replicas of those in the *paese*, were brought
from Italy at considerable expense. The origins of many Italian
churches are to be found in the rustic chapels which such
societies established to provide a setting for the cult of the saints.
Since this was often done without ecclesiastical permission, con-
flicts with the bishops followed over the question of ownership of
the churches. As Italian parishes were established, a struggle was
sure to ensue among various groups of *paesani* over the primacy
of competing patron saints. Should the church be named after San
Giuseppe or San Antonio? Which statue should be at the main
altar? The dispute was sometimes resolved by naming the church
after a neutral saint. One could determine the regional composi-
tion of an Italian parish by the saints and madonnas who were
venerated there. At times there would be a half-dozen images of
different madonnas about the altar, each the object of devotion of
a particular group of *paesani*.[13]

The cult of the patron saint was perhaps the strongest emotional bond, outside the family, which tied the immigrants to each
other and to the distant *paese*. Not surprisingly then, the *festa*
was the most vital and vivid expression of Italian immigrant culture in America. As Phyllis H. Williams observed, "Practically

every American town with an Italian community of any size and wealth observes one or more occasions of this nature, with the saints chosen that represent the largest homeland groups."[14] Despite the sneers of cynics, the shock of Protestants, and the embarrassed protest of Catholics, the *contadini* insisted on re-enacting these spectacles of medieval pageantry.

The *paesani* took great pains to replicate the *festa* as they had known it in the home town. Weeks of preparation created a sense of high excitement in the Italian neighborhoods, while a novena participated in by the women generated a mood of religious fervor. Dressed in "American" suits, adorned with sashes and other insignia, the sponsoring society attended Mass as a body (for some, the only day in the year they set foot in church). The priest delivered the panegyric invoking the protection of the saint upon the members of the society "from every imaginable evil." At the precise moment of the consecration of the host, torpedoes were exploded outside the church. Then the procession paraded the streets of "Little Italy," which were decked out with side-walk altars, food stands, vendors of sacred and profane objects, and arches of electric lights (these replaced the torches of the *paese*). The statue, carried by those who had bid the highest for the privilege, was accompanied by the sodality with banners fly-ing, a band, and hundreds (thousands in the larger cities) of devotees, many bearing large candles, barefoot, some on their knees. As the statue wended its way through the streets, the de-vout pinned money to its robes, virtually covering it with green-backs. For the believers, these were acts of piety; for the skeptics, it was a scandalous display of superstition.[15]

In America as in Italy, the *festa* was a patriotic manifesta-tion which by its re-enactment affirmed a symbolic unity with the *paese*. Here, if anything, with the representation of many dif-ferent town groups in one city, the competition in the magnifi-cence of the observances was even keener. Also the greater pros-perity permitted more extravagant displays. The mood of the *festa* as a day of recreation was captured by a contemporary description:

Everywhere whole families were out together, after the Italian custom, visiting, laughing, buying Italian sweetmeats, indulging in penny slices of watermelon, or applauding the familiar airs from Italian operas, played by the band stationed beside the church. Here too, a licensed gambling wheel drew a big crowd, but the best part of the celebration was the pleasure of fathers and mothers and children. Last of all rockets shot upward into the dark, more "bombe" were exploded and the lanterns were put out—the "festa" was over, the morrow at hand, when labor would begin once more.[16]

The basis of the cult of the saints among the immigrants was the belief in the efficacy of their miraculous powers in the New World as in the Old. Long before jet aircraft, the *paesani* believed that in a matter of hours, the patron saint could respond to the appeal from America. As Rosa Casettari put it: "In the old time was more miracle than now, but I see lots of miracles in Chicago too. The Madonna and the saint, they all the time make miracle to help me out."[17] Women like Rosa expressed their piety in saying the rosary, attending novenas, and keeping the banks of candles before the statues ablaze. Reporting on his tour of Italian parishes in 1924, Monsignor Amleto G. Cicognani commented that thanks to the Italian immigrants the practice of lighting candles had become widespread in all America. In the Italian churches the sale of candles was a major source of revenue, "almost every church, no matter how small, collects from four to ten thousand dollars a year, and even more." Within the Italian immigrant home, a minature shrine with images, statues, and crosses, lit by a flickering votive lamp, provided yet another focus for daily devotions.[18]

Although women were more conspicuous in their piety, Italian men were also among the petitioners of the saints. Among the miraculous cures and graces obtained through the intercession of Santa Maria Maddalena De-Pazzi in Philadelphia, which the Reverend Antonio Isoleri reported, were not a few involving men. The following is somewhat unusual:

Alfonso G. ——, about 45 years old, had been imprisoned on a very serious charge, and was then acquitted. After having been set free, he was fired at five times, but escaped unhurt. On the 29th of May, 1898 at 9 o'clock Mass, barefooted, on his knees, with his tongue on the floor, he dragged himself up from the main church door to the sanctury railing, in fulfillment of a vow for deliverance, acquittal, and escape, through the intercession of S. Mary Magdalen, who, he said, appeared to him in the prison the night after he made the vow . . . and bowed to him, as if to say, "Thy request is granted."[19]

This form of penance, *lingua strascinuni* (dragging tongue), was also practiced in Italy.[20] Other vows made in return for graces received, reported by Isoleri, included walking barefoot in the saint's procession, having Masses said in honor of the saint, and especially gifts of gold rings to the saint. Along with the cult of the saints, the immigrants brought with them their occult beliefs and practices. As Charlotte Gower Chapman discovered in Milocca, "Emigration does not free one from the power of witches. The men who have been in America bring back tales of their activities there."[21] If saints could make the trans-Atlantic crossing during the night, so could evil spirits. In Roseto, Pennsylvania, Carla Bianco was told of the woman from the Abruzzi who came to America as a ghost to see if her husband was sleeping with another woman. An old woman whose eldest son had married against her will sent a curse from Calabria to Chicago which caused his first-born to wither and die. Precautions then had to be taken against the evil eye; amulets were worn, rituals performed, and incantations chanted to fend off the power of witches. Meanwhile, in the Italian settlements, the *mago* and *strega* practiced their magic arts in behalf of the lovelorn, the vengeful, and the grief-stricken. As Alice Hamilton, who knew the Italian colony of Chicago intimately, observed: "Without the help of these mysterious and powerful magicians they believe that they would be defenseless before terrors that the police and the doctor and even the priest cannot cope with."[22]

To the outsider such beliefs appeared either ridiculous or sinister, but the *contadini*'s folk religion sustained them in difficult and even tragic circumstances. Confronted by strange and intractable situations in this new land, they clung all the more to their "tried and true ways of coping with the Great Unknown." The shared world view also reinforced the *contadini*'s sense of community. Each life crisis was faced with the support and participation of relatives and *paesani*. Funerals, for example, were communal experiences. Family and friends came from afar to share in the grief and to assuage it with food, drink, and talk. The ritualized outpouring of sorrow, the funeral laments, the tearing of hair, and the embracing and kissing of the corpse served as a catharsis. Traditional practices designed to pacify the soul of the deceased, such as the placing of objects in the casket, were followed. Prescribed forms and periods of mourning were observed. The religious culture of the immigrants, in short, strengthened their sense of identity and community and confirmed their human personality in the face of an existence which often appeared to deny their humanity.[23]

For the practice of their religion, the Italian immigrants were subjected to a torrent of insults and abuse. Denounced as benighted heathens, they were besieged by their self-appointed saviors, who offered to them the one true gospel of Christian (or Catholic) Americanization. The immigrants had come in quest of a better living; they submitted to untold hardships to achieve this end. If they wished to celebrate their *feste,* of what concern should this have been to anyone else? But in the evangelical climate of turn-of-the-century America, the spiritual state of the Italian suddenly became everybody's business. The Catholic Church and the Protestant denominations were engaged in a titanic struggle for dominance in America's cities, and the souls of the Italians became the chief bone of contention.[24]

American Protestants viewed the Italians as a priest-ridden people denied the true light of the Word of God and thus doomed to spiritual death. Divine providence had brought at least some of them to America so that they might be saved. To the middle-class Protestant with his confusion of social respectability, personal hygiene, and holiness, the poor, dirty Italians were surely under the power of Satan. Various denominations took up this challenge and expended large sums of money for ministers, Sunday schools, and settlement houses for the Italians. Several decades of such sustained effort yielded a mere handful of converts. The Protestant crusade to evangelize the Italians had failed.[25]

While the Protestant reaction was predictable, one might have expected a more sympathetic response from the Catholic Church. The bigotry of the American Catholics, however, equaled if it did not surpass that of the Protestants. No doubt the Italians failed to measure up to the norms of American—that is, Irish—Catholicism. The American Catholic was above all supposed to be respectful and obedient toward the clergy, faithful in attendance at Mass and in partaking of the sacraments, and generous toward the Church. Judged by such criteria, the Italian was no Catholic at all. Rather, as certain Irish priests declared, his religion was all emotionalism and external display. The *feste* of the Italians particularly scandalized the Irish Catholics. Strenuous efforts were made by the bishops in various dioceses to suppress the street processions, but to no avail. If denied the use of the church and the offices of the priest, the society would erect an altar on a vacant lot and hire a Protestant minister or defrocked priest to deliver the homily. Yet the threat of Protestant proselytizing and schism forced the Church to moderate its opposition to the peculiar piety of the Southern Italians.[26]

Viewing this clash of cultural traditions, some believed that ethnic parishes and Italian priests were essential to counteract the alienation of the immigrants from the Church in America. One of the most eloquent champions of the Italians, the Reverend Aurelio Palmieri, indicted the American Church for its lack of tolerance of the distinctive religio-cultural traditions of the *contadini*. Citing cases of flagrant bigotry on the part of Irish pastors, Palmieri called for the provision of Italian priests, who would understand and respect the religious sensibility of the Southern Italians.[27] With time, a considerable number of Italian national parishes were established in the major areas of immigrant settlement. Silvano Tomasi has argued that the ethnic parish by accepting the religious folklore of the immigrants served as an agent of group solidarity and unification of the Italians. He depicts the Italian priests as mediators between the established ecclesiastical structures and the peasant faith of the immigrants. Yet as Tomasi himself recognizes, the relationships between the Italian pastor and his flock were not always harmonious. The Italian priest was in the unenviable position of seeking to mediate between two very different worlds "with the risk," as Tomasi puts it, "of being shot by *paesani* or of being excommunicated by the Bishops."[28] Most of the Italian priests, moreover, came from the northern regions of the peninsula and found the mentality of the Southern Italians completely alien. A young priest from Tuscany assigned to a Sicilian parish in Chicago exclaimed: "Can these people be Italians?" The Reverend Giacomo Gambera, a missionary from Brescia, complained to his superior about his Southern Italian parishioners, declaring that the cult of the saints seemed to him "a pagan survival with only a change of idols."[29]

One of the recurring causes of conflict between Italian priests and parishioners was the disposition of the proceeds of the *feste*. As in Italy, the festival was sponsored by a lay committee which

made the preparations, hired the church and the priest, and
received the gifts of the faithful—presumably to cover the
expenses of the *festa*. But in America, it was said such committees were often controlled by unsavory characters who pocketed
the profits. When the priests sought to gain control of the *feste*
and of the contributions, they were subjected to threats, physical
assaults, and even attempts on their lives. Was the issue one of
the priests seeking to reclaim the *feste* for the Church from
racketeers who were trafficking in sacred goods? Or was the issue
one of institutional versus community control of a traditional religious celebration?[30]

Surely the emergence of a new generation of Italian-American
priests would bridge the chasm between the religious traditions of
the *paese* and the norms of American Catholicism. But vocations
were relatively few among the second generation, and those who
entered the priesthood were for the most part schooled at diocesan seminaries. Here they underwent a process of assimilation
to the dominant Catholic model from which they usually emerged
enthusiastic Americanizers. The Reverend John V. Tolino, for
many years pastor of the Church of the Annunciation in
Philadelphia, may serve as the archetype of the Italian-American
priest. Philadelphia-born of parents from Avellino (in Southern
Italy), Tolino was educated at the diocesan seminary. A dedicated priest and efficient administrator, Tolino believed that "the
burden of assimilating into full American life the aliens who come
to our shores . . . is . . . the work of the Church in America."
He enthusiastically implemented Dennis Cardinal Dougherty's
program to achieve this end among the Italians in Philadelphia.
Tolino advocated religious instruction particularly through the
parochial schools as the principal means of bringing the second
generation into the mainstream of American Catholic life.[31]

Tolino regarded the Italian emphasis on the cult of the saints as
"dangerously bordering on superstition." In his own parish, he
denied recognition to the societies devoted to local saints and
prohibited the traditional *feste*. On occasion Tolino intercepted
the processions and preached his denunciation in the streets. The
response of the Italians was to accuse Tolino of being an Irishman
with an assumed Italian name. Although Tolino may have been a
more zealous reformer than most, other Italian-American priests

of his generation seem to have shared his assimilationist ideology.[32]

The American Church was overwhelmingly hostile to the folk Catholicism of the Italian immigrants, so much is clear. What then became of the religious culture of the *contadini?* What has survived the unrelenting onslaught upon their "sacred cosmos"? Is there any such thing as an Italian-American Catholicism today?

The findings of recent studies of the religious behavior of Italian-Americans are inconclusive and at times contradictory. One school of thought has argued that the Italians have become increasingly like the Irish Catholics. This "Hibernization thesis" was first advanced by Will Herberg as a corollary of his "triple melting pot" conception of American society; the Italians and other Catholic ethnics were being assimilated into the Catholic "pot," which had a predominantly Irish flavor. Nathan Glazer and Daniel Patrick Moynihan took up this theme in *Beyond the Melting Pot,* concluding that as the Italians attained middle-class status their religious behavior tended to conform to the disciplined regularity of Irish patterns. On a theoretical level, Francis X. Femminella hypothesized that a significant segment of the Italians had in fact "internalized" Irish-American religious values. But he also suggested that many Italians had "withdrawn" from the hostility of the Irish Church, not rejecting Catholicism, but refusing to assimilate the Irish Catholic norms. From this response of indifference Femminella conjectures the possibility of "a positive Italian influence on American Catholicism."[33]

A more substantial study based on survey data was conducted by Nicholas John Russo of the religious acculturation of Italians in New York City.[34] Russo concludes rather cheerfully that in religious practices and attitudes the longer the Italians are in America the more they tend to be like Irish Catholics. However, his own data are contradictory on this very point. In terms of certain religious practices, the second- and even more the third-generation Italians do seem to be approaching the Irish Catholic norm (for instance, supporting the Church financially, sending children to Catholic schools). They also seem to be moving away from Italian religious customs (for instance, honoring the patron saints, lighting candles, and praying more to the Virgin and saints

than to God). However, on the sacramental index, attendance at
Mass, reception of Holy Communion, and confession, the significant discrepancy between Irish and Italian behavior is not only
maintained in the second and third generations, but even
increases. From the Russo study, one could conclude that if the
distinctive qualities of Italian Catholicism are being washed out in
the second and third generations, still the Italian-Americans are
not moving toward the Irish Catholic model. If anything, the data
suggest that their behavior is best described by Femminella's
concept of "indifference."

A more recent study of ethnic diversity in American Catholicism, also based on survey data, tends to confirm the continuity
of the pattern of indifference with respect to formal religious
practices on the part of Italian-Americans of all generations. Using Mass attendance, Communion reception, and parochial
school support as indices of religious involvement, Harold
Abramson concluded that "generation itself has no influence on
Italian religious behavior; indifferent levels of activity persist."
On all of these measures, the Italians tended to rank at the bottom
of the scale along with the "Spanish-speaking" as compared to
other Catholic ethnic groups. To the question: "Have Italian
Catholics become Irish?" Abramson's answer was no, with the
possible exception of the minority who marry outside the ethnic
group.[35]

How much of the folk religion of their ancestors have the
Italian-Americans retained in their spiritual life? Has the cult of
the saints, for example, been entirely eradicated by the strenuous
efforts to secure uniformity of worship in the Church? As men-
tioned above, Russo's study suggests a waning of traditional devotional practices; for example, while 57.8 percent of first-
generation respondents reported praying more to the Virgin and
the saints than to God, only 29 percent of the second and 22.6
percent of the third admitted doing so. In his recent work,
*L'America degli Italiani,* the Reverend Alberto Giovannetti
commented that the removal of the statues of patron saints from
the churches, those statues brought with such love and sacrifice
from Italy, indicated that the grandchildren of the immigrants had
lost the traditional piety of their forefathers.[36] However, having
visited Italian churches in various parts of the country during the

past year, I can attest to the fact that the statues are there,
removed from the main altar perhaps, but there—San Rocco,
Santa Lucia, la Madonna del Carmine, and others, with banks of
candles burning before them. Efforts to remove the statues from
certain churches have sparked protests:

When the Irish pastor decided to renovate the sanctuary according to the
modern liturgy of the Roman Catholic faith, part of that change meant
eliminating the devotional candles and statues that Italo-Americans held
dear to them. When the priest found out that some of the influential and
wealthy Italians would leave the parish, he very quickly dropped the
idea.[37]

The sacristan of a large Italian church on the West Coast told me
that if the statues were removed, the church would have to be
closed. He also volunteered the information that the parish took
in more money from the sale of candles than from collections at
Masses. As in older times, the devotion to the saints is privately
conducted in the home as well. One can find in luxurious
suburban ranch houses, as well as modest city apartments, a
shrine with images and statues of the Madonna and saints.

The most dramatic manifestation of the continuing vitality of
the cult of the saints is the celebration of the *feste,* which in fact
appear to have taken on a new lease on life in recent years. As the
multiple identities of the hundreds of groups of *paesani* have
merged into a general Italian-American identity, so too the devotions to the multitude of local patrons have merged into the cult of
a few favored saints and madonnas. Dispersed residence and the
automobile make possible the gathering of thousands for the
popular *feste* of la Madonna del Carmine in Melrose Park,
Illinois, and in Hammonton, New Jersey, and of San Gennaro in
Greenwich Village. In cities around the country many of the
*paesani* societies still sponsor the feast of their patron; in 1976,
the Riciglianesi of Chicago, for example, observed the *festa* of
Santa Maria Incoronata for the eighty-first consecutive year.
These celebrations retain much of the traditional character with
Masses in honor of the patron, street processions, bands,
barefoot women carrying candles, and fireworks.[38] But what is
left of the original piety? Aside from the social aspects of the *feste*
(always important), what remains of the faith in the miraculous
power of the saints and madonnas?

And what of the occult which was such an integral part of the immigrants' folk religion? With the current revival of interest in witchcraft and demonology, American culture appears to be catching up with the *contadini* of a century ago. Those Italian-Americans who in the rush to assimilate rejected the wisdom of their grandmothers are out of phase again. Yet the knowledge and practice of magic have not disappeared among the second and third generations. In her study of Roseto, Pennsylvania, Bianco found that "beneath the evident adjustment to certain aspects of American life, a whole world of traditional values, folk beliefs, and fantasies persists, in some ways as rich as that the immigrants left behind them in the Old Country."[39] A few years ago, Elizabeth Mathias discovered that South Philadelphia's Italians continued to follow many folk religious practices, particularly relating to sickness and death, while they derided these beliefs as superstitions. The belief in the evil eye remains common even among the third generation; the *corno* (horn of gold or coral) is still worn often along with a religious medal under the shirt, even by educated professional men.[40] Incantations are used to cure headaches and to solve other problems. Bianco's report of the cure of the evil eye by recitation of the magic formula over the telephone has been confirmed by other informants. In the Italian neighborhoods, one can still find practioners of the magic arts. Rene Cremona of Cleveland was having a string of bad luck with his business. On the advice of his neighbors, he consulted "a woman with the blessing" to get rid of the *mal'occhio*. The *maga*, Lena DeCapua, second vice president of the Ohio State Catholic War Veterans Ladies Auxillary, had learned to cast out spells from her grandmother. Mrs. DeCapua said that she received several calls a week from people requesting help. Cremona said: "Scientifically I don't understand it. But I'm taking it seriously because I see how seriously so many other people around here take it."[41] Four decades ago, Phyllis Williams cautioned against "the popular idea . . . that superstition can swiftly be eradicated by a joint program of Americanization and education. Such deep-seated customs, if swept aside at all, are dissipated gradually."[42]

How widespread are such survivals of both cult and occult in Italian-American Catholicism? The evidence of survivals cited is admittedly impressionistic and fragmentary. Contrary evidence exists as well. Certainly, as Russo's data suggest, traditional devotional practices are being observed less frequently among second and successive generations. What is more signigicant is Bianco's observation that the communal context within which the folk religion survived and was transmitted is itself disappearing. Increasingly life is becoming more a private affair and less a shared experience. This trend is discernable in the changing Italian-American funeral practices. What had been a set of rituals for dealing with death, including the custom of night wakes and funeral lamentations, has been largely discarded. As Mathias writes: "The padded luxury of the funeral parlor has become the scene for the drama of the last hours with the body of the deceased, and the funeral director has taken over the duties which had once been performed in the peasant culture by the family alone."[43] Decorum and restraint have replaced the weeping and wailing of yesteryear. Here indeed the Italians appear to be approaching the Irish Catholic model. Russo reported that while 68.4 percent of the first-generation Italians admitted reacting emotionally at funerals, only 59 percent of the second generation, and 37.3 percent of the third generation did so (the Irish scored 31.5 percent). Other traditional practices have been prescribed by the Church. The use of bands at funerals and photographs on the tombstones were recently, for example, banned. According to the undertakers, the reason for such changes was "uniformity, we're striving for uniformity."[44]

The study of the fate of Italian folk religion provides an illuminating perspective on the history of the Catholic Church in America. In this light, the Church emerges as one of the major agencies of "Americanization," pursuing the objective of total, if gradual, assimilation. Early in this century the American hierarchy appears to have espoused the managerial ideology of seeking optimum institutional efficiency through the standardization of the religious behavior of all Catholics. One wonders whether the prelates were familiar with Frederick Winslow Taylor's ideas of scientific management; certainly they reflected the spirit of his thought. Just as in the factories the bodies of the Italian workers were subjected to a discipline alien to their ethnic character, so the Church sought to impose upon their spirits the

model of the "good American Catholic." Ironically by allying itself with the forces of rationalization and bureaucratization, the
Church facilitated the process of secularization which has eroded
so deeply modern man's capacity for religious faith. The Italian
immigrants brought with them an ancient religious culture, a
Mediterranean sensibility pervaded by mysticism and passion.
The American Church rejected this gift, to its and their great loss.

## Notes

1. For a full discussion of the controversy regarding the "Italian
Problem," see the author's "Prelates and Peasants: Italian Immigrants
and the Catholic Church," *Journal of Social History,* 2 (Spring 1969),
217–268.
2. Until recently American Catholic historiography has paid little attention to the religious experience of the laity. Its traditional focus had
been upon the clergy and the institutional Church. The popular piety of
various Catholic ethnic groups is only now beginning to be studied. A
recent example of this kind of "history from the inside out" is Jay P.
Dolan, *The Immigrant Church: New York's Irish and German Catholics,
1815–1865* (Baltimore, 1975). Studies which deal with the religious behavior of Italian immigrants are: Harold J. Abramson, *Ethnic Diversity in
Catholic America* (New York, 1973); Silvano M. Tomasi, *Piety and
Power: The Rise of Italian Parishes in the New York Metropolitan Area*
(Staten Island, N.Y., 1975); and Richard A. Varbero, "Philadelphia's
South Italians and the Irish Church: A History of Cultural Conflict," in
*The Religious Experience of Italian Americans*, ed. Silvano M. Tomasi,
*Proceedings of the American Italian Historical Association*, Sixth Annual Conf., 1973, pp. 33–52.
3. The term is Thomas Luckmann's, who defines it as the domain of
reality where "both the ultimate significance of everyday life and the
meaning of extraordinary experiences are located." *The Invisible Religion* (New York, 1967), p. 58.
4. These generalizations are not meant to imply that Southern Italy
was culturally homogeneous. Regional and local variations in religious
beliefs and practices were common. Yet ethnographic and historical
studies suggest that in the large the Southern Italian peasants did have a
common world view. It should also be noted that many elements of this
world view were shared by the agricultural populations of Central and
Northern Italy. For a review of the Italian literature on the religious life
of the South see Lucilla Rami, "Religiosità e Magia nel Sud," *Socio-
logia; Rivista di Studi Sociali* (Rome), 6 (September 1972), 95–145. Also

useful in this respect is *La Religiosità Meridionale, Selezione CSER 6–7* (Rome, June–July 1972). Among a growing number of studies, the most important are Ernesto de Martino, *Sud e magia* (Milan, 1966) and Gabriele De Rosa, *Vescovi, popolo e magia nel Sud* (Naples, 1971).

5. An older but basic work is Phyllis H. Williams, *South Italian Folkways in Europe and America* (New Haven, 1938); see particularly pp. 135–139. The most vivid description of the peasant mentality is still to be found in Carlo Levi, *Christ Stopped at Eboli* (New York, 1947).

6. The folk religion of the *contadini* can be studied through the many anthropological reports on villages of Southern Italy; among the most useful of these are: Charlotte Gower Chapman, *Milocca a Sicilian Village* (Cambridge, Mass., 1971); Ann Cornelisen, *Torregreca. Life, Death, Miracles* (New York, 1970); A. L. Maraspini, *The Study of an Italian Village* (Paris, 1968). Since these studies were conducted following the period of mass immigration to the United States, the persistence of traditional religious patterns is all the more striking. For a review of the anthropological literature see Leonard W. Moss and Eugene Cohen, "Where are we now: an inventory of recent research," *The Stephen C. Cappannari Memorial Symposium; New Directions in Anthropological Research in Italy* (mimeographed, 1974).

7. Maraspini, *Italian Village,* pp. 226–227; on the cult of the saints, see also Williams, *South Italian Folkways,* pp. 135–139; *La Religiosità Meridionale,* pp. 18–20.

8. For an excellent description of a *festa* see Norman Douglas, *Old Calabria* (New York, n.d.), pp. 201–212; also Chapman, *Milocca a Sicilian Village,* pp. 158–180; Levi, *Christ Stopped at Eboli,* pp. 117–120.

9. George R. Gilkey, "Italian Emigrant Letters. The *Teramesi* Write Home from America," trans. from Filippo Lussana, *Lettere di illetterati* (Bologna, 1913) [unpub. MS in Immigration History Research Center, University of Minn.]. The increased expenditures the *feste* made possible by immigrants' gifts has also been noted by Prof. William A. Douglass in his study of Agnone, Molise. Private communication, Oct. 14, 1975.

10. Cornelisen, *Torregreca,* p. 256.

11. Leonard W. Moss and Stephen C. Cappannari, "Folklore and Medicine in an Italian Village," *Journal of American Folklore,* 73 (April 1960), 85–102; Chapman, *Milocca a Sicilian Village,* pp. 196–207; Williams, *South Italian Folkways,* pp. 141–158; Cornelisen, *Torregreca,* pp. 243–263.

12. Carla Bianco, *The Two Rosetos* (Bloomington, 1974), p. 85; Jerre Mangione, *Mount Allegro* (New York, 1963), p. 105.

13. Noting this phenomenon, Tomasi maintained that it was the function of the Italian ethnic church to incorporate and fuse "into one com-

munity the fragmented Italian immigrants of the same American neighborhood.'' By bringing the village cults of the saints together in the same church, the ethnic parish ''brought about an internal process of universalization.'' *Piety and Power,* pp. 97, 124–125, 168. See also Vecoli, ''Prelates and Peasants,'' p. 231.

14. Williams, *South Italian Folkways,* p. 149.

15. The *feste* were described in detail in the Italian-American press. During the summer months, almost every issue carried accounts of one or more *feste. L'Italia* (Chicago), Aug. 24, 1901. Tomasi cites expressions of opposition to the *feste* in *Piety and Power,* pp. 123–125. An anticlerical view of the *feste* was presented by Olindo Marzulli, *Gl'Italiani di Essex* (Newark, N.J., 1911), pp. 29–30: ''The faithful element among the immigrants has brought here its patron saints and with them all the hometown forms of the cult. Every village of Southern Italy has here a *società operaia* which celebrates its patron. And when the *festa* cannot be made in America, money is collected so that it can be celebrated in the village, since the pastor incites the faithful to turn to their relatives in America so that they will not forget to honor with their money the old saint and the young madonna from whom they have always received the grace of a holy protection. And the *contadini,* who have not yet been able to pay off their own debts, hurry to send the fruits of their labor so that they can be converted into smoke and trinkets to offer to the saint. Here there is an active contest among the different societies, each of which seeks to overshadow the others in magnificence of the celebration. The solemn choreography of the processions of our villages is exactly reproduced, except for the greater effort due to the greater prosperity. There is a saint who, when he is carried in the procession, is literally covered with paper money. Even towards the saints the sympathies of our people run from indifference to fanaticism. And there is no reasoning which is able to convince them of the folly of these external forms of the cult which are ridiculed even by American Catholics. In fact these celebrations serve only one purpose: that of causing our people to be considered very boisterous and more enamored of the externals of the faith than of the faith itself. Nor is there hope that these religious processions will end as long as the old generations are alive.''

16. ''Celebrating a Feast Day,'' *By Archer Road* (Chicago), 3 (Sept. 1909).

17. Marie Hall Ets, *Rosa, the Life of an Italian Immigrant* (Minneapolis, 1970), p. 242.

18. Monsignor Amleto G. Cicognani, ''Visita Apostolica agli Scalabriniani degli Stati Uniti d'America (settembre–ottobre 1924)'' in ''Stati Uniti e Canada Ovest Provincia San Giovanni Battista Visite Can-

oniche," Archivio Generale, Pia Società dei Missionari di S. Carlo, Rome. On the home shrines, see Bianco, *Rosetos,* pp. 87–88.

19. Antonio Isoleri, "Special Graces and Favors attesting the Devotion to St. M. M. De-Pazzi in Philadelphia," *Souvenir and Bouquet ossia Ricordo della Solenne Consecrazione della Chiesa Nuova di S. Maria Maddalena De-Pazzi* (Philadelphia, 1911), pp. 76–84. Father Isoleri noted: "Here we relate a few of the many occurrences of what may be regarded as miraculous cures and graces, obtained through the intercession of the Saint; though, mindful of the decree of His Holiness Pope Urban VIII and of the Sacred Congregation of Rites, we claim nothing more for them than a purely human and historical authority."

20. Chapman reports this practice: *Milocca a Sicilian Village,* p. 160.

21. Ibid., pp. 203–204.

22. Bianco, *Rosetos,* p. 92; Alice Hamilton, "Witchcraft in West Polk Street," *American Mercury,* 10 (Jan. 1927), 71. See also Anna Zaloha, "A Study of the Persistence of Italian Customs among 143 Families of Italian Descent" (unpub. master's thesis, Northwestern University, 1937).

23. Williams, *South Italian Folkways,* p. 159; Zaloha, "Italian Customs," pp. 155, 168–171. On Italian-American funeral practices see Elizabeth Mathias, "The Italian-American Funeral: Persistence through Change," *Western Folklore,* 33 (1974), 35–50. The author observes: "One of the most notable features of the funeral of the South Philadelphia Italian-American community is the persistence of a South Italian village funeral pattern." A personal reminiscence of Italian-American wakes is Rose Grieco, "Those Who Mourn," *The Commonweal,* 57 (March 27, 1953), 628–630.

24. Richard M. Linkh, *American Catholicism and European Immigrants (1900–1924)* (Staten Island, N.Y., 1975), which describes the attitudes and policies of the Church with respect to the Italians and other newcomers, stresses its relative ineffectiveness as an agency of Americanization. Linkh comments, however, (p. 190) that "when Catholics did undertake immigrant care on even a small scale, they seemed to be motivated not primarily by Christian charity, but more often than not by the discomforting thought that Protestants were winning the race for souls and making inroads in the traditionally Catholic population."

25. On Protestant efforts to proselytize among the Italians see Theodore Abel, *Protestant Home Missions to Catholic Immigrants* (New York, 1933); Tomasi, *Piety and Power,* pp. 47–50, 153–159; Vecoli, "Prelates and Peasants," 267–268; Angelo Olivieri, "Protestantism and Italian Immigration in Boston in late 19th century: The Mission of G. Conte," in Tomasi, ed., *The Religious Experience of Italian Americans,* pp. 73–103.

26. Tomasi, *Piety and Power,* pp. 44–47, 143–159; Vecoli, "Prelates and Peasants," pp. 243–248. During an extended polemic in *America,* one who signed himself "An Old Pastor" voiced his opinion of the Italians as follows: "Their religion, what there is of it, is exterior. Once I entered a big Italian church, in a big city, and while there many devotees came in to visit, as I first imagined, the Most Blessed Sacrament, but to my surprise and, will I say my disgust, their devotion consisted in lighting candles, prostrating themselves before statues, going from shrine to shrine, from side altar to side altar, sidetracking altogether the main altar wherein reposed the Savior of men." *America,* 12 (Dec. 19, 1914), 244.

27. Aurelio Palmieri, *Il grave problema religioso italiano negli Stati Uniti* (Florence, 1921); see also the Reverend J. Zarrilli, *A Prayerful Appeal to the American Hierarchy in behalf of the Italian Catholic Cause in the United States* (Two Harbors, Minn., 1924).

28. Tomasi, *Piety and Power,* p. 143.

29. Giacomo Gambera, "Autobiografia, Alcuni Ricordi di Vita Missionaria negli Stati Uniti d'America," Religosi Defunti, Archivio Generale, Pia Società dei Missionari di S. Carlo, Rome. Father Gambera received threats of death for his opposition to the promoters of the *feste* whom he suspected of crass motives.

30. Tomasi, *Piety and Power,* p. 141; *Chicago Daily Tribune,* Aug. 14, 1903; Edmund M. Dunne, *Memoirs of "Zi Pre"* (St. Louis, Mo., 1914), pp. 17–18. The Reverend Dunne, later Bishop of Peoria, was the first pastor of the Italian Guardian Angel Parish on Chicago's West Side.

31. Tolino expressed his views in a series of articles in *The Ecclesiastical Review,* "Solving the Italian Problem," 99 (Sept. 1938), 246–256; "The Church in America and the Italian Problem," 100 (Jan. 1939), 22–32; "The Future of the Italian-American Problem," 101 (Sept. 1939), 221–232.

32. Varbero, "Philadelphia's South Italians and the Irish Church"; Christa Ressmeyer Klein, "Catholicism in Southern Italy and in the Philadelphia National Parish: Its Sect-Like Characteristics" (unpub. seminar paper, University of Pennsylvania, 1968). I am indebted to Professor Varbero for making a copy of this paper available to me.

33. Will Herberg, *Protestant-Catholic-Jew* (Garden City, New York, 1955); Nathan Glazer and Daniel Patrick Moynihan, *Beyond the Melting Pot* (Cambridge, Mass., 1963); Francis X. Femminella, "The Impact of Italian Migration and American Catholicism," *The American Catholic Sociological Review,* 22 (Fall 1961), 233–241.

34. Nicholas John Russo, "The Religious Acculturation of the Italians in New York City" (unpub. doctoral dissertation, St. John's University, 1968); Russo summarized his findings in "Three Generations of Italians in New York City: Their Religious Acculturation," in *The Italian*

*Experience in the United States,* ed. by S. M. Tomasi and M. H. Engel (Staten Island, N.Y., 1970), pp. 195–209. Russo's research methodology is open to criticism on two grounds: 1) the questionnaires were distributed by priests in their parishes with resulting possibilities of bias in both sample and response; 2) the survey data do not distinguish between responses of males and females. Given the traditional differences in religious practices on the part of Italian men and women, the latter is a particularly serious limitation.

35. Harold J. Abramson, *Ethnic Diversity in Catholic America* (New York, 1973), pass.

36. Russo, "The Religious Acculturation of the Italians in New York City," p. 259; Alberto Giovannetti, *L'America degli Italiani* (Edizioni Paoline, 1975), p. 277. The Reverend Giovannetti concluded: "The Irish have won. The Italians of the third and fourth generations are today fully integrated in the modes of a Catholicism which is more or less molded after the Irish model."

37. Patricia Snyder Weibust, *The Italians in Their Homeland in America in Connecticut,* The Peoples of Connecticut Multicultural Ethnic Heritage Series Number Two (Storrs, Conn., 1976), p. 83. "In Connecticut, interviews with a number of Italians confirmed that, in their opinion, Italian Catholicism is still unique."

38. Reports on the *feste* can be followed in such publications as *Fra Noi* (Chicago) or *The National Italian American News* (New York).

39. Bianco, *Rosetos*, p. x.

40. Mathias, "The Italian-American Funeral," p. 44. Following the presentation of this lecture at St. Joseph's College in Philadelphia, I was approached by a well-dressed Italian-American gentleman who undid his collar and tie to show me a tiny gold horn and a crucifix on a chain. Gold amulets sell well in Philadelphia jewelry stores.

41. *The Plain Dealer* (Cleveland), Feb. 25, 1975.

42. Williams, *South Italian Folkways,* p. 158.

43. Mathias, "The Italian-American Funeral," p. 44; Bianco, *Rosetos,* pp. 118–120.

44. Russo, "The Religious Acculturation of the Italians in New York City," p. 263; Mathias, "The Italian-American Funeral," pp. 44–45.

# Chapter 3

# The Irish Catholics
## A Postponed Perspective

### Dennis J. Clark

It is ironic that historians of democracy have only recently begun to study the history of ordinary citizens.[1] This democratization of historical study has rescued that discipline from elitist presumptions and academic possessiveness, but the rescue can only be temporary. New forms of distortion are always available to replace the fashions of the older ones. Nevertheless, the current interest in ethnic studies and social history should greatly enlighten us about how this vast and complex nation has developed. The results of such study, if we are wise, should then teach us more about what we need to know about life, about how men behave, and about what forces from the past have impact on us today. In a time of considerable national doubt, bewilderment, and disillusionment, such rewards for study have a special significance precisely because they give occasion for reflection about ourselves.

The title of this chapter indicates that a review of the religious history of the Irish Catholics is overdue, postponed because of the difficulty that the task represents, and postponed because of how truncated much of the study of the subject has been in the past. Yet the size of the subject demonstrates its importance. The Irish Catholics have played a vital role in the history of parliamentary democracy, both English and North American. They

were distinctive participants in the Atlantic migration that proved
so central to the development of a number of the world's leading
modernized countries. Moreover, the international network of
social, nationalist, and religious affiliations that so influenced
the settlement, urbanization, and cultural growth of several
continents has been maintained even in the modern age.[2] As a
result the Irish have lived among and interacted with peoples of
other nations while retaining their own consciences and hearts.
This interaction between the Irish Catholic spirit and a larger non-
Irish society is the subject of this chapter. The broad question is:
What do we know about the religious response of Irish Catholic
people to the novelty, complexity, and social challenge of the
American life?

The most extensive explorations of Catholic history in the
Americas relate to the diffusion of Spanish, Portuguese, and
French Catholics in the ages of discovery and settlement.[3] The
French experience, at first boldly missionary, then largely
isolated by the waning of French colonialism, has implications
that are still emerging in Canada. The Iberian religious involvement with colonialism and Indian and African cultures is a mo-
mentous subject that is increasingly attracting study. But the extraordinary religious mingling in the United States is perhaps the
most difficult to understand, for it involved not only a hugely
varied Protestant and sectarian spectrum, but Catholics from a
dozen major European ethnic traditions. Examination of this
unique development may prove helpful in understanding Catholic
life in the United States because the Irish Catholics have played a
key role in America's religious history and had a special potential
for social interaction in the country.[4]

It is estimated that the Irish immigration to the United States,
including entries during colonial times, totals some nine million
people. Of these, about nine-tenths were probably of Roman
Catholic background.[5] This massive Irish influx, concentrated
most heavily in the nineteenth century, had a broadly formative
influence upon American Catholicism as a whole, and a mod-
erating and delimiting influence upon other American religions as well. After increasing in the 1830s, Irish immigration
became a flood following the Great Famine of 1846–47. The
number of Catholics in the country increased from 300,000 in

1830 to 3,000,000 in 1860, and this growth was predominantly Irish.[6] The increase coincided with American developments of major cultural significance. The re-awakening of Protestant evangelical spirit, especially in the 1840s, meant that Catholicism would encounter a renewed and highly volatile Protestantism different from the limited membership churches of colonial times. Also, Irish concentration in the new cities of America during the period of America's most rapid city growth meant that Irish Catholics would have to deal with their religious problems in the novel context of radical urbanization.[7] Thus, the timing of the major Irish influx dictated some important elements in the religious adjustment process.

The increase in sectarianism and denominational independence in the nineteenth century also made for more voluntarism among Protestant churches. The Irish Catholics, because they had been deprived of state patronage and aristocratic philanthropy in Ireland, were also disposed toward a voluntarist conduct of their church development. The ordinary member of the parish was the chief resource for its support.[8] This was a far cry from the European Catholic tradition and added to the distinctiveness of the American Catholic evolution. Because of Protestant hostility and because of the voluntarist impulse, the Irish Catholics were led to build a whole parallel system of social and educational institutions that created both social segregation and a thriving group life. This, in turn, stimulated and ratified pluralist differences in American society on a much larger scale than had been the case at the nation's outset. The Irish Catholics were the largest single group prior to the Civil War to test actively the constitutional mandate for pluralism. Moreover, they were able to establish a relatively successful *modus vivendi* with the general society, a resolution that neither blacks nor Indians were able to achieve in the nineteenth century.

The religious and socio-political formula of the Irish Catholics would serve other immigrant groups well, but not without friction and special adaptations for each group. Sam Bass Warner says that one of the results of this formula was that American public education became secularized in reaction to the alternative of serving as an interreligious battleground.[9] The sources of secularization, however, were much more diverse. At a crucial time

the Irish Catholic group, the largest ethnic element of America's
largest single church for generations, made an imprint in a creative manner on the nation's religious life. They did this from the
bottom of American society and against many disabilities. This
was a new achievement for Catholicism, and an innovation for
American life that was not enacted without keen stress and
resistance to all that it implied.

But to assess the ethnic and spiritual forces behind this Irish
achievement is a most difficult matter. One problem is the sheer
extent of the Irish-American experience itself. It is simply
enormous and has not drawn sufficient research to clarify ade-
quately its stages and diversity. In colonial times Irish redemp-
tioners and indentured servants broke their indentures with
alacrity, and largely without regard to the ties of religion. The
prominent Irish Catholics in the American Revolution period
were adventurers, magnates, and Whigs, and were largely conscious of their class position far above the indentured commoners
who shared their faith.[10] The refugees from the famine and
distress of the 1820s and 1830s, and from the calamitous Great
Famine of 1846–47, were refugees in the starkest sense. David
Miller and Emmet Larkin have shown how very weak their religious organization was according to modern expectations.[11] As
will be illustrated below, the post-famine generations were of different social background. Changes in Irish education, church organization, and mores made for a different kind of emigrant. Finally, the modern Irish immigrants from 1890 to the present were
the beneficiaries of the religious building that had gone on before.
Their attitudes and sense of worth were strongly affected by the
religious achievements of their immediate predecessors. Such a
great expanse of social and religious experience cannot be easily
summarized, however.

Aside from the generalizations already set forth above, which
are manifest in the Catholic establishment and public posture that
exists today, we know only a little of how this broad development
occurred. In addition to covering a lengthy span of time, the Irish
influx spread widely in America. States like Wisconsin felt its impact early; cities beyond the Eastern seaboard such as New
Orleans and St. Louis had large numbers by 1860; and frontier
towns, numerous mining towns, and St. Patrick, Missouri and

Garryowen, Iowa were founded by them.[12] The problem in studying such a group is to pay keen attention to locality, sequence,
and regional differences. The scholar must foster an exploratory
and even controversial approach to offset the omissions and easy
assumptions with which the subject has been afflicted. A primary
difficulty has been the sanctimonious and self-serving distortions
of Irish and Catholic history penned by those too bemused or
dishonest to accord people and events what they deserve first—
realistic and critical portrayal. So much pious nonsense and
wretched whitewash has been cascaded on this subject that it will
be generations before we know the character of much of it.

Further, the studies that we do have offer a very limited excur-
sion into this enormous field. Major American historians have not
devoted much attention to it. Among historians and others who
have examined the Irish-Catholics there exist wide diversions of
judgment. Older historians such as John Gilmary Shea and
Philadelphia's own Peter Guilday accorded the group a central
role in American Catholic development. Father Thomas
McAvoy, however, assigns them a much more limited role and
concedes the primary role to English Catholics with colonial
roots. Oscar Handlin, focusing on social mobility and general
contributions to urban life, characterized the group as stricken
and haplessly limited after immigration and slow to adapt to the
United States. David Doyle of University College, Dublin em-
phasizes the later immigrants in the 1880s and 1890s and sees
them as mobile, competent, and led by men of high achievement.
Joseph O'Grady, John B. Duff, and others differ about the extent
to which the group has affected American foreign policy toward
Ireland. Concerned with the persistence of group identity and
values, Father Andrew Greeley perceives a massive erosion of
Irish-American identity, while my own work stresses the very
long history of the group as a fixture of American ethnic difference and the many changes that it has undergone over the
course of American history.[13] Thus, if the historians differ, we
need not be too shy about advancing our own assertions amid the
contradictions. The opposing views may not be immediately
resolvable, but the conditions prompting them should be understandable. In this spirit, let us begin to explore the Irish Catholic
past and presence, alluding to Philadelphia for illustrations.

Ireland prior to 1850 gave little promise of the social and religious "empire" (as it was sometimes called) that would later develop overseas. The incredible poverty, shattered culture, continuous exploitation, periodic famine, and resulting degradation of the island were much more likely to produce social and religious disorder than a tidy Catholic peasant culture similar to those idealized in Europe. Indeed, "peasantry" implies some control of labor and land. The Irish controlled neither. They did not even control their own misery. Irish Catholicism, made licit again by Catholic emancipation in 1829, was recovering from two centuries of devastation. It had an evolving educational and ecclesiastical framework and strong aspirations but its organization touched only about one-third of the impoverished, rural population. Church administration was in frequent disarray. There was a shortage of priests, churches, and leadership. The traditional allegiance of the people to Catholicism was partly composed of belief in central doctrinal ideas, partly superstitious devotion, partly a folk-consciousness of a great tradition that had once been, and partly a commitment to vindicate Catholicism as one element of a suppressed nationalism. This background was a highly unlikely seed bed for the growth of America's largest denomination.[14]

The slow emergence of effective Irish national consciousness and religious security, however, generated an astonishing church expansion after the Great Famine of 1846–47. Church building, vocations to religious life, devotional regularity, and missionary zeal flourished against great odds.[15] The tragedies of the period from 1700 to 1850 had deprived the Irish people of many of the normal outlets for social development. The Church with its potential for elaboration and service became a central vehicle for Irish energies. For a multitude of Irish people it became *the* culture, *the* standard for social reference, *the* dominant local institution. The newness, or what could be called the renewed character, of this church experience gave it a spirit of enterprise, a plasticity, and the allegiance of a mass following that made it especially pertinent to American conditions in the second half of the nineteenth century where a similar constructive period was underway. Long repressed, Irish religious organizing ability surged in Ireland and the United States after 1850.[16]

The ties of Ireland to the American Catholic Church involved first a massive immigrant infusion, but also a strong tradition of migration by Irish priests and nuns, intense opposition to Protestant evangelism, and a commitment to voluntarism for religious activity both in Ireland and the United States. In both countries these latter qualities would be profoundly important for Church history.

This Irish Catholic religious disposition was thrust into American life on a large scale beginning in the 1830s and 1840s. The cultural shock of trying to adjust to massive immigration was great, but at the same time American life on the Eastern seaboard was agitated by other extensive changes. Urbanization was taking place at a very rapid pace. Old leadership patterns were being challenged. The new mass democracy that arose in Jacksonian times was struggling for political definition and control. And Protestantism, the dominant religion, was enlivened by a powerful wave of revivalism and evangelical activity. This latter force insured that the incoming Irish Catholics would encounter a Protestantism bent on defending the Sabbath, campaigning for temperance, and insisting upon its right to proselytize and uphold Protestant mores. Indeed, anti-Catholic publishing was widespread.[17]

These conditions mandated conflict. The Irish Catholics were too large a group to be driven west like the Indians, too diffused to be harassed directly as a group like the Mormons, too intractable to be kept as slaves or even indentured servants. The most notable example of anti-Irish rioting, that in Philadelphia in 1844, occurred prior to the Great Famine influx. With the Irish presence growing year by year, the only feasible policy for thoughtful Protestants was to hope for partial social segregation and some improvement in the future. The more superheated evangels, however, were determined to keep the pressure on Irish Catholics, to divert them, subvert them, or convert them.[18]

The swiftly changing urban economics and population patterns enabled the Irish to distribute themselves through the cities in two generations after 1840. Economic opportunities gave the Irish communities sufficient affluence to create their own middle class. The Church itself was a great system for educational diversification. While the Irish were excluded from certain social circles, they compensated by building their own network of parishes, schools, organizations, fraternities, labor unions, political groups, seminaries, and social patterns in an extraordinary outburst of creative energy. Their very social disabilities became the occasion for constructive work as hospitals, orphanages, reformatories, temperance halls, homes for the elderly, and hospices proliferated. As early as the 1850s, prominent Irishmen were living in fashionable areas of Philadelphia, small Irish businesses were thriving, and the parishes in the city were beginning to show clear class differences in their congregations.[19]

In a structural sense the cities offered the Irish new orbits of social experience. Residential neighborhoods were far flung and diversified as the newcomers gradually overcame poverty. The labor market was varied, changing, and full of innovations as the Industrial Revolution created whole new industries. Grade schools, academies, high schools, trade schools, night schools, apprenticeships, self-improvement societies, and dozens of other media coaxed the newcomer toward broader education. Unparalleled freedom of association, popular literacy, and the abundant novelty of city life stimulated immigrant curiosity and attainment. The contrast of this range of urban outlets with the limitations of Irish rural life drew generations to American cities in a propulsive cycle of industrialized emigration.

The concentration of the Irish in urban districts led to the location of Catholic strength in those areas that were the very seats of rising industrialism. It was the cities that were the learning centers of America, not the prairies. It was the cities that became the crucibles of diversity, not the rural hinterlands still dominated by early settler stock. Urbanization opened to Catholicism the panorama of change required to adapt it to American conditions. The rural "Bible Belts" might remain intolerant and inhospitable, but the cities placed Catholics in the vitals of the American process, and it was the Irish Catholics who, as immigrants, first traced their careers in this new environment in journalism, medicine, law, politics, teaching, and in thousands of humble callings.

The time-frame in which this Irish Catholic development took place is important. Between 1830 and 1860 twenty-three new parishes were organized in Philadelphia, most under Irish sponsorship. Around these the schools and other facilities grew. The collections to support the seminary and charity work became regularized. The Catholic newspaper, reorganized in 1866, drew an even wider readership. Catholic bookshops grew in number. By 1880 the original four parishes of the city existing in 1830 had grown to forty-one. Although German Catholics were strongly organized, the Irish were much more broadly responsible for this church development as is clear from the lists of the clergy and congregations.[20]

What had emerged from this period was something quite novel, a popularly based and supported Catholic structure without government or aristocratic aid. It was a structure at grips with practical issues of education and social problems far different in scale and scope from those that preoccupied bishops in Ireland. The American Irish were dealing with problems in an urban context and in a rapidly changing free society. Ireland was rural, still oppressed, and changing only slowly. The American Irish were undergoing a process of modernization in religion and lifestyle at a swift pace. They were entering the "Achieving Society" with its new goals, use of time, and technology. This new society brought new needs to these Irish immigrants, a new kind of struggle for survival, the challenge of new conditions that required experiments, and new institutions.

While those in the old country still worried about crops, land, and the annual visit of the priest to say Mass at the whitewashed, thatched-roofed cottage, the American Irish fretted over labor unions and strikes, the possibility of secondary education for their children, and the temptations of the big city. While church administration in Ireland remained in old-fashioned albeit revitalized molds, the American Irish launched innovations on a large scale in building their independent parish schools, medical facilities, colleges, libraries, and financial systems.[21] Although voluntarism was the key to their system, it was gradually being organized in a most American pattern of efficiency with committees of all kinds, reports, diocesan land banks, seminary recruiting drives, and missionary funds.

One feature of the robust Catholicism after 1850 both in Ireland and the United States was a relentless drive to regularize teaching religion and worship. Catechisms, manuals of rubrics, pre-printed sermons, and routinized parish functions became the religious counterpart of the mass production systems that had taken over work life. Along with a blizzard of devotional tracts and practices, most of them saccharine, stilted, and dull, this movement brought a truly American belief in the virtues of mechanization into religious practice. The American experience had to be ordered to be tolerable to the catechetical mentality of Catholic leadership, and so it was energetically compartmentalized into a complex of theological, pastoral, and moral categories. The effect of this process, and of the adaption to an urban environment cut off from the cycle of the seasons, was to all but obliterate the folk religion that the Irish had brought with them to America. The homely compound of simple beliefs, rural rituals, and moral adages was now replaced by a complicated overlay of memorized formulas, rote prayers, stereotyped devotional methods, and arbitrary regulations.[22] This devotional change was the popular imitation of the disciplined performances that had been drilled into the clergy by Reformed seminary training. The discourse with eternity was routinized and made to run on time like the great American railroads whose tracks ran off into the horizon and beyond to infinity.

Behind this great Catholic church emergence were certain forces—the stimuli or formative influences—impelling the movement in the nineteenth century and even the twentieth. Sufficient allusion has been made thus far to the religious outlook of the Irish to indicate that the traits of the group and the popular memory and resilience among the Irish contributed much to the building of their church in America. Beyond this, however, the position of the Irish in American society, especially from 1830 to 1880, deeply affected their religious development. As a largely alien, stigmatized, exploited, and impoverished minority group, their lower-class position placed them in social jeopardy. The resulting partial segregation and difficult relations with the dominant Anglo-culture strongly shaped Catholic activity. E. Digby Baltzell and others have described how the upper-class Philadelphia Protestants systematically excluded Catholics, Jews, and others from social leadership in the nineteenth century. The city's prestigious cricket clubs, learned institutions, and fashionable recreations were carefully modelled on British lines,

and the Irish Catholics were not welcome no matter how successful they became. This situation produced for the Irish Catholics
qualities of independence, privatism, and cultural isolation that
would require generations to change.[23]

Another major influence was the recurrence of controversy
that attended Irish Catholic development. As much as the
inheritance from Ireland and the class position of most of the
faithful, controversy shaped the Irish mind.

In Philadelphia the "trusteeism" dispute beginning in the 1820s
among trustees of St. Mary's Church left a legacy of acrimony
and suspicion that affected the diocese greatly. That the dispute
was especially linked to the Irish community is evidenced by the
fact that the two newspapers founded to trade broadsides in the
affray were called *The Catholic Advocate and Irishman's Journal*
and *The Irishman and Weekly Review*. The debates over local
support for Daniel O'Connell's Repeal movement in the 1840s
generated strong anti-Irish opinions expressed in such verses as:

> Bogtrotters are made Alderman
> Who can barely read or seal,
> They damn our laws and shout aloud
> For Ireland and Repeal

> They worship Dan O'Connell
> And feed his greedy hands
> With cash drained from our citizens
> And then they damn our land.

The Fenian revolutionary efforts of the 1860s led Archbishop
James Wood to issue a circular letter to other bishops condemning what he saw as an unholy conspiracy of terrorists. The Land
League of the 1880s was seen by many as a conspiracy against
private property sprung from the radical "single tax" gospel of
Henry George. The 1916 rising in Dublin that forecast Ireland's
war for independence was greeted in the Catholic press in
Philadelphia with stern condemnation. All these controversies
echoed on the local level roiling Irish Catholic differences.[24]

Despite this petulant and beset posture, the Irish Catholics certainly could not entirely segregate themselves from the spirit and
ideas of the society around them. They were deeply affected by
the Victorian mores of the basically Protestant society surround-

ing them. The ideas of general middle-class propriety became
their ideas as they aspired to middle-class status. This was especially true among leaders and churchmen who felt compelled to
be socially respectable. The Victorian Protestant ideas about sex,
the family, deportment, and religious dignity and reputation had a
trenchant impact upon the Irish. The Irish, coming from a rural
background, were seeking a new popular ethic for their new city
life. They needed rules to guide themselves and to prove their
Americanism, their solidity, and their virtuosity. The widely discussed puritanical streak in Irish Catholicism is much more a
result of English and American Protestant influence than a
product of traditional Irish rural life, where the nature of sex was
more casually regarded. The romantic attraction of ritual to Victorians and the stoic yet strenuous quality of Victorian religion
had a strong influence on Irish Catholics in the United States.
Increased literacy, the expectations of others, and the Irish-
American window on upper-class standards provided by generations of duty as servants—English-speaking servents—all
contributed to the propagation of Victorian mores. These mores
were embraced by "lace curtain" Irish leadership. (Within living
memory most rectories in Philadelphia had carefully hung lace
curtains.)[25]

The thousands of Irish Catholics who became middle-class in
the 1880s moved to ornate Victorian houses in West Philadelphia,
Oak Lane, and Germantown. They sent their daughters to
convent schools which studiously observed the prudery of the
Victorian cult of female incarceration. They had their own
coteries and literary salons in which Maurice Francis Egan,
Eleanor Donnelly, and Martin I. J. Griffin held forth. To view
their stiff-collared and brocaded photographs in the old files of
the *Records* of the American Catholic Historical Society is to
view the very essence of Victorian respectability.

Finally, the elaboration of religious activities was affected by
the need of the Irish-Americans for a system that was their own, a
system that was a vehicle for mobility, orientation, and prestige.
Lacking any real government in the old country and hindered by
prejudice in the new, the Irish in the United States were at first
unable to obtain high ranking posts in the American government.
The Church became the channel for the exercise of talent

otherwise excluded from various areas of American life. In addition, it was a system with its own law, regulations, and administrative structure. As such it possessed an extensive network with many of the characteristics of bureaucracy, and bureaucracies, private and public, would be one of the signal features of life in the twentieth century. The Irish Catholics became adept at church bureaucracy as readily as they would later become functionaries of government bureaucracy. The managerial ethic among the Irish-Catholic churchmen became a characteristic of the "brick-and-mortar" bishops and priests whose church careers paralleled the bureaucratic careers of their relatives in secular structures.[26] The bishop, the political boss, and the corporate executive were not strangers. They mirrored one another in their cultural preoccupations with building, organizing, and fitting others into functional roles in their networks of prestige and power. Only the bishops had higher mandates for their roles.

Philadelphia prelates like Archbishop Patrick J. Ryan left a legacy of vigorous administration that would have its impact on the twentieth century. Dennis Cardinal Dougherty for four decades tended and expanded the Archdiocese with relentless commitment. His business administration of church holdings was prodigious and notably successful, resulting in a land bank estimated at $1.5 billion in 1965. Cardinal Dougherty was the embodiment of the churchman with business skills. The Victorian success model lingered on. John Cardinal O'Hara, the son of a small businessman, spent years as the head of the Business School at the University of Notre Dame before becoming an archbishop and cardinal.

The increasing use of official statements, Archdiocesan office buildings, and the mass media all reflect the Irish Catholic transition from folk religion to ecclesiastical bureaucracy. It has not come without some cost. The studied avoidance of involvement in the tragedy of Northern Ireland between 1969 and 1976 on the part of Irish-American churchmen is a testimony to the chilling caution that is inherent in church bureaucracy. Though the Ulster situation is full of pitfalls, the needs of the Irish Catholics and Protestants in that area cry out for non-partisan outside aid and succor. With only a few exceptions, however, the Irish Catholic churchmen in the United States have been mute in the face of this latest trauma in Ireland, a nation still marked by the ravages of colonialism.

To summarize the points about the influences shaping Irish Catholicism in the United States: The Irish Americans were not, as the stereotype had it, intoxicated with whiskey in the nineteenth century so much as they were intoxicated with religion. Yet the Irish in Ireland prior to 1850 were not a very Roman Catholic people. Rather, they were Irish Catholic according to their own folk religion traditions. The church they erected in the United States was, however, not especially Irish. It was Irish-American, preoccupied with urban change and opportunity, and quite different from that of Ireland. It was ethnocentric, but Catholic and American. Despite terrible Protestant-Catholic confrontations, Protestants played a major part in shaping this American Irish Catholic Church in that the mores of Protestant Victorians exercised a powerful influence on the Irish-American clergy and bourgeoisie. Finally, if America's business was business, this same business produced "business bishops" as the clergy with vows of poverty became increasingly adept at the managerial ethic.

If all this abounds in contradictions, I hope they are sufficiently interesting to tempt scholars to devote more study to the subject. The subject does indeed need further study, for it is central to our understanding of how our pluralist society came to be, how our cities were organized, and how that compound of confidence and achievement comprising the American "spirit" grew and strengthened itself. We need to know in just what ways Irish experience affected American leadership and popular attitudes about group differences, poverty and community organization, and the seizing of opportunities for employment, education, and religious development. Now that the focus of American studies has shifted somewhat away from who got here first, who proclaimed the Anglo-Saxon credo of eminence, and who attained prominence, we can expand the study to that profoundly important question of democratic inquiry: "What forces shaped the daily life of the people, and how did they respond?"

Notes

1. With respect to scholarly interest in Irish Catholics in Philadelphia, it is significant that the *Pennsylvania Magazine of History and Biography* in the years between 1910 and 1970 published over 900 articles. Of these less than 10 percent dealt with the nineteenth and twentieth centuries, when the Irish population was a huge social fact. Only eight articles could be said to be devoted to Irishmen, and several of these were about Irish Protestants. The *Records* of the American Catholic Historical Society of Philadelphia succeeded in arrogating Irish Catholic material to its pages. The religious partition of historical study has been impressively thorough and regrettably long lasting.

2. On the seventeenth- and eighteenth-century Irish emigration see Maurice Hennessey, *The Wild Geese* (New York, 1974). A perusal of Edward Machysaght's *Irish Families* (New York, 1957) illustrates the prominence of Irishmen in Europe, Latin America, and Australia as well as the United States.

3. There is no counterpart for the Irish of the classic works of the Jesuit *Relations,* the works of Francis Parkman, or the studies of Edmundo O'Gorman and other Latin American historians. The two most widely available histories of the Irish in the United States, Carl Wittke, *The Irish in America* (Baton Rouge, 1956) and William V. Shannon, *The American Irish* (New York, 1963), are surveys. Wittke gives a factual summary of the Irish role in the Church. Shannon contrasts the careers of Father Charles E. Coughlin and Monsignor John A. Ryan.

4. This neglect of study of the Irish Catholic is part of the larger default of study of Catholic life generally by the American historians. See Philip Gleason, ed., *Catholicism in America* (New York, 1970), pp. 1–9.

5. Irish immigration 1820 to 1850 is estimated at 4.6 million. Oscar Handlin, ed., *Immigration as a Factor in American History* (Englewood Cliffs, N.J., 1959), p. 16. Estimates of Americans of Irish ancestry range to 16 million.

6. Carl Wittke, "Immigration Policy Prior to World War I," in Benjamin M. Ziegler, ed., *Immigration: An American Dilemma* (Boston, 1953), p. 3.

7. I have pursued this question at some length in Dennis Clark. *The Irish in Philadelphia: Ten Generations of Urban Experience* (Philadelphia, 1974), pass.

8. For religious conditions in the United States during this period of initial heavy immigration see Timothy Smith, *Revivalism and Social Reform: American Protestantism on the Eve of the Civil War* (New York, 1957); Ray Allen Billington, *The Protestant Crusade* (Chicago, 1964). For a broad treatment see Thomas P. O'Neill and Raymond H.

Schmandt, *History of the Catholic Church* (Milwaukee, 1965), pp. 605–610. *The Metropolitan Catholic Almanac,* pub. first by F. Lucas in Baltimore (1850), later by John Murphy and Co., gives relevant statistics.

9. Sam Bass Warner Jr., *The Urban Wilderness: A History of the American City* (New York, 1972), p. 165. Although religious segregation did grow, Thomas O'Dea says the Irish were particularly influential in Americanizing the European-conditioned Catholic Church because the Irish were plebian, democratic, and anti-monarchical. Thomas F. O'Dea, *Sociology and the Study of Religion* (New York, 1970), pp. 75–76.

10. Michael J. O'Brien, *A Hidden Phase of American History* (New York, 1920). The class background in Ireland was described by Thomas D'Arcy McGee, *The Irish Settlers in North America* (Boston, 1852), p. 234; and Daniel Corkery, "Davis and the National Language," in M. J. MacManus, ed., *Thomas Davis and Young Ireland* (Dublin, 1945), p. 15.

11. David Miller, "Irish Catholicism and the Great Famine," *Journal of Social History,* 9 (Fall, 1975), 81–98; Emmet Larkin, "The Devotional Revolution in Ireland, 1850–75," *American Historical Review,* 77 (June 1972), 625–652. The voluntarism characteristic of Irish Catholicism is noted by Donald H. Akenson, *The Church of Ireland: Ecclesiastical Reform and Revolution, 1800–1885* (New Haven, 1971).

12. Maldwyn Allen Jones, *American Immigration* (Chicago, 1960), p. 121. For a regional distribution see Franklin D. Scott, *The Peopling of America* (Washington, D.C., 1972), p. 39. James P. Shannon, *Catholic Colonization on the Western Frontier* (New Haven, 1957); and Sister M. Justille McDonald, *The History of the Irish in Wisconsin in the Nineteenth Century* (Washington, D.C., 1954) discuss the West. Robert Emmet Kennedy, *The Irish: Emigration, Marriage, Fertility* (Berkeley, 1973), p. 82 gives urban estimates. The process of protracted change involved with Irish-American immigration and adjustment is revealed in Joseph P. O'Grady's *How the Irish Became Americans* (New York, 1973).

13. See Gleason, ed., *Catholicism in America,* pp. 6–7; John Tracy Ellis, *Perspectives in American Catholicism* (Baltimore, 1963), pp. 45–50; Peter Guilday, *The Life and Times of John Carroll, Archbishop of Baltimore* (New York, 1922); Father Thomas McAvoy, "The Formation of the Catholic Minority in the U.S., 1820–1860," *The Review of Politics,* 10 (January 1948), 13–24; David Doyle, "American Immigrant Communities: A Critique of New England Models with Special Reference to Irish America in 1890–1900," paper delivered at the British Association of American Studies, Hull, England (Mar. 30, 1974). Doyle contrasts with Oscar Handlin, *Boston's Immigrants* (New York, 1969). Joseph P. O'Grady, "Irish-American and Anglo-American Relations, 1880–1918" (unpub. doctoral dissertation, University of Pennsylvania, 1965); and

John B. Duff, "The Versailles Treaty and the Irish Americans," *Journal of American History,* 55 (Dec. 1968), 582–598. Andrew M. Greeley, "The Last of the Irish Fade Away," *New York Sunday Times,* Mar. 14, 1971, and the same author's *That Most Distressful Nation: The Taming of the American Irish* (Chicago, 1972) contrast with Clark, *The Irish in Philadelphia.*

I have been most encouraged to read a book published in 1975, *The Immigrant Church: New York's Irish and German Catholics, 1815–1865* (Baltimore, 1975) by Jay P. Dolan, which takes a social history approach to the study of parishes in New York City. The book is a keenly researched attempt to discern the forces shaping the immigrant religious experience. The sources are largely related to direct religious affairs, and data on such social influences as employment, housing, and family life is not central to the study. One reservation about this fine study is that Dolan narrowly construes the forces acting on the Catholic parishes, so that ecclesiastical influences are accorded more weight than is proper. As with my own studies of Philadelphia Irish communities, however, Dolan finds considerably more diversity than has been heretofore credited to the immigrant communities. He also sees the religious background of the immigrants in terms of the privation that undercut formal religious practices in the old country. He notes as well the controversies in which the Irish were involved, especially those with the German Catholics and the Protestant mainstream groups. He sees the increase of Church property as giving rise to a "brick and mortar priest." He traces the rise of the authoritarian style of episcopal dominance, calling it "boss rule," a term that approximates my own conclusions about the bureaucratic style of Catholic churchmen.

Dolan's book is a salutary and refreshing analysis of the evolution of American Catholicism. I am pleased to say that we reached our respective conclusions independently. I did not read his fine book until I had written this paper, which is why this rather long note is placed in the chapter notes. One could discuss Dolan's book profitably in great detail. Its importance for this paper is that it confirms many of the points I have advanced.

14. Larkin, "The Devotional Revolution in Ireland, 1850–75"; Miller, "Irish Catholicism and the Great Famine"; Gearoid O'Tuathaigh, *Ireland Before the Famine, 1798–1848* (Dublin, 1972), pp. 42–74; E. R. Norman, *The Catholic Church and Ireland in the Age of Rebellion, 1859–1873* (Ithaca, N.Y., 1965).

15. Joseph Lee, *The Modernization of Irish Society, 1848–1918* (Dublin, 1973), pp. 42–48; Larkin, "The Devotional Revolution in Ireland, 1850–75, " pp. 635–645.

16. Patrick Egan, "The Influence of the Irish on the Catholic Church

in America in the Nineteenth Century," The O'Donnell Lecture, National University of Ireland, (June 14, 1968). For a listing of Church growth in Philadelphia, see Joseph L. J. Kirlin, *Catholicity in Philadelphia*, (Philadelphia, 1909).

17. Marcus Lee Hansen, *The Immigrant in American History* (New York, 1964), pp. 97–128; Billington, *The Protestant Crusade*, pp. 53–197; Henry F. May, *Protestant Churches and Industrial America* (New York, 1949), pp. 3–38; C. S. Griffin, *The Ferment of Reform, 1830–1860* (New York, 1967).

18. The Irish from colonial times forward were the group with the worst records as servants and escaped most readily from indentures: Richard B. Morris, *Government and Labor in Early America* (New York, 1965), p. 288. Michael Feldberg, *The Philadelphia Riots of 1844* (Westport, Conn., 1975), puts the riots in perspective as part of the general violence of disrupted early industrial cities.

19. Clark, *The Irish in Philadelphia*, pp. 88–125; John Tracy Ellis, *American Catholicism* (Chicago, 1969), p. 89, says that by 1866 there were 45 prelates Irish-born or of Irish descent. This Irish prominence in the Church was seen as quite regrettable by intellectuals such as Isaac Hecker and Orestes Brownson. See Daniel Callahan, *The Mind of the Catholic Layman* (New York, 1963), pp. 38–51. Yet the careers of such men as Thomas D'Arcy McGee and John Boyle O'Reilly were "streaked with ambivalence" as Thomas Brown has noted, as they strove to adapt to American ways instead of imposing Irish ones. By 1866 at the Second Plenary Council, a whole new generation of Irish-American clergy with a distinct American outlook was at hand. Thomas N. Brown, "The Irish Layman," and Thomas T. McAvoy, "The Irish Clergyman," in *A History of Irish Catholicism*, 6 (Dublin, 1970), 22 and 94.

20. Dennis Clark, "A Pattern of Urban Growth: Residential Development and Church Location in Philadelphia," *Records* of the American Catholic Historical Society, 82 (Sept. 1971), 159–170. See the multitude of names in Joseph L. Kirlin, *Catholicity in Philadelphia*, (Philadelphia, 1909). Insight into parish life is given in Joseph P. Barrett, *The Sesqui-Centennial History of St. Denis Parish* (Havertown, Pa., 1975). This book is probably the best parish history in the United States because of its social view, its illustrations, and its attention to detail. It is a remarkable record of an Irish Catholic community. The study of Irish Catholic social mobility has been extended in recent years by the work of statistically oriented historians, such as Stephan Thernstrom, *The Other Bostonians* (Cambridge, 1973); Bruce Laurie, Theodore Hershberg, and George Alter, "Immigrants and Industry: The Philadelphia Experience, 1850–1880," paper delivered at the Sixth International Congress on Economic History, Copenhagen, Denmark (Aug. 19–23, 1974); and Andrew

M. Greeley in his work at the National Opinion Research Center in Chicago.

21. The scale of operations in a city like Philadelphia by 1895 was impressive with 183 churches and 12 buildings, 411 priests, 98 parish schools, 1,600 nuns, and 415,000 Catholics. See Daniel H. Mahoney, *Historical Sketches of the Catholic Churches and Institutions of Philadelphia* (Philadelphia, 1895). For the growth of schools see Thomas J. Donaghy, F.S.C., *Philadelphia's Finest: A History of Education in the Archdiocese of Philadelphia* (Philadelphia, 1972).

22. There is no adequate library of this devotional material. The Archives of the American Catholic Historical Society at St. Charles Seminary, Overbrook, Pa., contains examples, however. A mood of optimism straining for perfectability inhabited America and led to minute care of obligations: Irving Bartlett, *The American Mind in the Mid-Nineteenth Century* (New York, 1967), pp. 38–40. Even in 1848 the visiting evangelist George Lewis was impressed by American morality: George Lewis, *Impressions of America and the American Churches* (Edinburgh, 1848), p. 103.

23. Early in the nineteenth century the Irish in Philadelphia were deeply preoccupied with the threat of proselytizing Protestantism. *The Catholic Herald* claimed 100,000 Irish children "were lost to the church." Donaghy, *Philadelphia's Finest,* p. 64. This fear of religious conversion remained prominent for generations. Promotion of Catholic schools was fueled by it. See *The School Question: Catholics and Education* (New York, 1876), pp. 28–49. Bishop John Hughes considered his immigrant flock to be worse off and more vulnerable than the black slaves: Hugh Nolan, *The Most Reverend Francis Patrick Kenrick, Third Bishop of Philadelphia, 1830–1851* (Philadelphia, 1948), p. 307. E. Digby Baltzell, *Philadelphia Gentlemen* (Glencoe, Ill., 1958); Sam Bass Warner Jr., *The Private City: Philadelphia in Three Periods of Its Growth* (Philadelphia, 1968) tells of the "privatism" that became a social characteristic of the city.

24. These stanzas are from the Reverend Arthur J. Ennis, *Old St. Augustine's Catholic Church* (Philadelphia, 1965), p. 36. For the "Hogan Schism" and Trusteeism see Francis E. Tourscher, *The Hogan Schism and Trustee Troubles: 1820–1829* (Philadelphia, 1930). For the Repeal Association see Feldberg, *The Philadelphia Riots of 1844,* pp. 27–30. For the Fenian Movement see Dennis Clark, "Militants of the 1860s: The Philadelphia Fenians," *The Pennsylvania Magazine of History and Biography,* 95 (Jan. 1971), 98–108. Some economic views in the Land League frightened moderates: Thomas N. Brown, *Irish-American Nationalism* (Philadelphia, 1966), pp. 121–123. The effect initially of the

1916 Dublin rising was to alarm *The Catholic Standard and Times* (Philadelphia): Catherine McGinley, "Irish-Americans in Philadelphia and Their Involvement with the Irish Independence Movement" (paper presented at a history department seminar, Temple University, 1966). Added to this history of disputes was the long currency of derogatory images of the Irish Catholics as inferior, irrational, and criminal: L. P. Curtis, *Apes and Angels* (Washington, D.C., 1971).

25. For the characteristics of Victorian religion see David Daiches, *Some Late Victorian Attitudes* (New York, 1969), pp. 17–19; Desmond Bowen, *The Idea of the Victorian Church: A Study of the Church of England, 1833–1889* (Montreal, 1968). The attraction of formal ritualism for Victorians is noted by E. R. Norman, *Anti-Catholicism in Victorian England* (London, 1968), p. 105. The difference between the superstitions of folk religion observed by T. Croften Croker, *Researches in the South of Ireland* (New York, 1968, first pub. 1824) and the customs and beliefs documented by Sean O'Suilleabhean, *Irish Wake Amusements* (Cork, 1967), and the massive dignity of ceremonies in the new Cathedral of Sts. Peter and Paul in Philadelphia in 1864 is impressive. Mahoney, *Historical Sketches,* pp. 28–29. The cultivation of formality became a popular craze. O'Dea finds formalism to be a chief characteristic of American Catholicism: Thomas F. O'Dea, *American Catholic Dilemma: An Inquiry into Intellectual Life,* (New York, 1958), pp. 155–158. The Irish remain the ethnic group most committed to formal observance: Harold J. Abramson, *Ethnic Diversity in Catholic America* (New York, 1973), p. 108.

The conservatism of United States Catholicism throughout its history is noted by Brown and McAvoy, *A History of Irish Catholicism,* Vol. 6, pass. This conservatism accorded well with the period of Irish dominance in the Gilded Age and after. Desmond Fennell, *The Changing Face of Catholic Ireland* (Washington, D.C., 1968) argues that the stereotypes of a prudish, authoritarian, intellectually arid Irish Catholicism are false. He finds the chief characteristics of nineteenth-century Irish Catholicism to be close lay-clergy relations, views favoring church-state separation, belief in liberal democracy, progressive ideas on land problems, and a revolutionary streak. All these were present, of course, but the relative weight and impact of each is unclear.

The rural conservatism of Irish people toward formal sex arrangements was part of a realism about sex and marriage that was traditional. The disaster of the Famine introduced a rigid code of restriction due to the bitter problems of poverty and land transfer that influenced marriage decisions. The puritanical reserve of Irish Catholicism, though economic in origin, was greatly accentuated by the Victorian cults of romanticism and deportment. K. H. Connell, *Irish Peasant Society* (Oxford, 1968), pp. 113–162. The tracing of these attitudes to French Jansenist influence is tendentious.

26. Catholics appear disproportionately in bureaucratic roles in American life: Melvin L. Kohn, "Bureaucratic Men: A Portrait and an Interpretation," *American Sociological Review*, 36 (June 1971), 461–475. Bureaucrats tend to be urban, to have a good educational background, and to have faith in structured systems. The administrative and financial role of Church leaders was a natural result of the mass organization tasks undertaken by American Catholicism. Callahan, *The Mind of the Catholic Layman*, pp. 144–145. Edward Levine, *The Irish and Irish Politicians* (Notre Dame, 1966) discerns an Irish Catholic group preoccupation with power and its use. One scholar finds an ethic of rewards guiding Irish politics: Terry N. Clark, "The Irish and the Spirit of Patronage," *Ethnicity*, 2 (1975), 305–359. Emmet Larkin sees the cultural interaction of church and culture in Ireland as laying the bureaucratic basis and comprehension for the modern Irish state: Emmet Larkin, *The Roman Catholic Church and the Creation of the Modern Irish State, 1848–1876* (Philadelphia, 1975). The careers of such men as John Cardinal O'Hara who succeeded Dennis Cardinal Dougherty were deeply involved with business associations and business education: Thomas T. McAvoy, *Father O'Hara of Notre Dame: The Cardinal Archbishop of Philadelphia* (Notre Dame, 1967). It is not accidental that the Archdiocese of John Cardinal Krol is today a leader in Church administration with its new office building and extensive property.

Chapter 4

# Philadelphia and the German Catholic Community

Jay P. Dolan

The history of German-American Catholicism began more than two hundred years ago. Long before the Revolution of 1776 the Gospel was preached to German Catholics in their mother tongue, especially in Pennsylvania, where two-thirds of the Catholic population in 1757 was German. However, the number of Catholics in colonial America was small, so meager in fact that John Adams observed that in his home town a Catholic was about as "rare as a comet or an earthquake." But if you wanted to find a Catholic in colonial America, and in particular a German-speaking Catholic, a good place to look was Philadelphia.[1]

German-speaking and English-speaking Catholics had worshiped together in St. Joseph's Church and later at St. Mary's Church before the Revolution. Yet the small band of German Catholics was already showing a sense of distinctive group consciousness in the eighteenth century. In 1768 they purchased their own burial ground, and it was evident that the separation of Catholics along lines of nationality was beginning to develop. In 1787 Germans organized the German Catholic Society and informed John Carroll, then Prefect Apostolic of the United States, that in order "to keep up their respective nation and Language" they were "fully determined to build and erect another new place of divine worship for the better convenience and accommodation

69

of Catholics of all nations particularly the Germans under whose direction the building was to be constructed."[2] Two years later, the new church, Holy Trinity, was opened for service. In organizing their own church the Philadelphia Germans gained the distinction of founding the first national parish in the United States; the subsequent history of Holy Trinity illustrates how difficult and contentious such a development would be. From the very beginning German Catholics had to do battle with Church authorities who desired both an American church that knew no national distinctions and an hierarchically structured church that recognized no lay authority in ecclesiastical affairs. The hierarchy lost the battle against the national parish, but they ultimately won the war by gaining control of the system of lay trusteeism.

Throughout the nineteenth century the German American Catholic community increased numerically in both Philadelphia and the nation, principally through large waves of immigration in the 1850s and the 1880s. In 1840 one of every ten Catholics in the United States was German (70,592 of 663,000). In the next thirty years, the German Catholic population increased fourteen times, and by 1870 about one of four Catholics was of German stock (1,044,711 of 4,504,000). The Catholic Church had become the single largest denomination in the country, and German Catholics were fast becoming the largest subgroup of church Germans. After the heavy immigration of the 1880s, the number of German Catholics increased to approximately two million by 1890, a 100 percent increase in twenty years.[3] Thereafter, a decline set in as immigration from German-speaking countries ebbed, and the descendents of earlier immigrants became less distinctively German. In 1916 only one of ten Catholics (1,672,670 of 15,721, 815) worshiped in a church that used the German language.[4] Despite the decrease in the German Catholic presence, they had the distinction of being the largest subgroup of church Germans, numbering "slightly less than the total membership of several German Protestant denominations."[5] Within the Catholic Church they were still the largest foreign-language group.

The dominance that German Catholics enjoyed in Philadelphia in the colonial period did not persist into the nineteenth century. By 1842, German Catholics had increased to approximately 12,000, or 20 to 25 percent of Philadelphia's Catholics (about 50,000). Proportionately this was a significant decline from the days when three out of five Catholics in Philadelphia were Germans. By the sheer force of numbers the Irish had gained control of the Church and the Germans had slipped back into second place. In the next fifty years the increase in the German Catholic community was slight. In 1869 they numbered 21,000; by 1892 a rough estimate would put their population at 35,000, or approximately 17 percent of Philadelphia's Catholic population.[6] More significantly, the German Catholic population represented only 3 percent of the city's population in 1890; the entire foreign-born German community equaled only 7 percent of the city's population.[7] What had happened is obvious from the hindsight of history. Like other Germans, Catholic Germans had bypassed Philadelphia in the nineteenth century and chose to settle elsewhere, principally in the Midwestern triangle bounded by the cities of Cincinnati, Milwaukee, and St. Louis. The story of German-American Catholicism, which began in Philadelphia in the eighteenth century, had shifted west following the flow of German immigrants.

In the nineteenth century German-American Catholics had become a minority population in Philadelphia. As Catholics they were outsiders in the larger Protestant culture of the city. As Germans they were a minority both in the city and the Church. To preserve their religion in an alien society and to preserve their ethnicity in an Irish church, they followed the patterns set by their colonial ancestors. They formed their own national parishes which, in the mind of one German priest, were "the best means to protect the Catholic immigrants against the loss of their faith, to safeguard them against the inducements and seductions of our adversaries, and to enable them to preserve incorrupt the sacred treasures of religion and to transmit it to their children."[8]

The national parish was the institutionalized attempt of an immigrant group to preserve the religious life of the old country. Among German Catholics it became a distinctive trademark in the nineteenth century. The heart of the issue was language. German Catholic immigrants came from many different countries in Western Europe, but they shared two common traits—language and religion. The two were inextricably joined together. "Language saves faith" was the slogan of German-American Catholics.

Reflecting this mentality, an immigrant guidebook advised

newly arrived Germans not to "settle in districts and places where there are no German priests, churches and schools."[9] To settle in an English-speaking parish was "the greatest of all dangers" since "experience teaches that even in places where there are English Catholic churches but no German-speaking priests, German Catholics will become indifferent to the Church within a short time and in due course will be even worse than Protestants and pagans."[10] To this author the English-speaking parish was as great a threat to the faith as a Methodist church. Loss of language meant loss of faith, and it did not matter how you lost the mother tongue, the outcome was inevitably the same. This heightened sense of ethnicity caused one observer to remark that the Germans wanted "everything in German and if they are ever obliged to have Irish or American priests, they complain loudly about this insult."[11]

This fear of the loss of faith, as extreme as it was, appeared to be justified. In Philadelphia, "that irreligious and immoral city," the vitality of religion in the German community was directly connected with the availability of German-speaking parishes. In 1840 the "greater number" of the German community lived in the upper part of the city, where rent was cheaper because of its "distance from the center of the city and because of the poverty of those sections." But the only German parish, Holy Trinity, was located in the lower part of the city. Even under the best of circumstances it could not serve the needs of Philadelphia's 12,000 German Catholics. Thus, many Germans appeared to have "fallen away from the Faith." In 1843 the church of St. Peter's was organized for the German Catholics who lived north of Vine Street in the upper part of the city. From the very beginning the parish began to attract German Catholics from this part of the city as well as from the suburbs of Kensington and North Liberty. According to one writer, the establishment of St. Peter's Church prompted "very many" German Catholics to return to "the one saving faith of their fathers which they had given up either in part or completely."[12] St. Peter's eventually became the showcase of German Catholicism in Philadelphia. By 1848 the congregation numbered 3,000; fifteen years later it was the largest German parish in the city with 10,000 people.[13] The same pattern occurred in the founding of St. Alphonsus Church. Because of trustee troubles, Holy Trinity parish was placed under an interdict and the church was closed. As a result, the Germans of South Philadelphia were without a church, and this caused a "great falling away from the Church."[14] To remedy the situation, the new parish of St. Alphonsus was organized in 1853.

The loss of faith among German immigrants was a serious problem. The most obvious index of this was participation in church services. Only 40 to 60 percent of the Catholic immigrants regularly attended church on Sunday, and many German Catholic immigrants received the sacraments every twenty, thirty, or even forty years. Another less tangible indicator was the decline, or even the absence, of religion itself among the immigrants. German observers noted that their countrymen were not only lax in practicing their religion, but were becoming indifferent as well—"religious only in appearance," as they described it. Others commented that "many had given up the Catholic faith; others were Catholic in name only." The lack of priests and churches deprived them of the support needed to keep the religion of the old country alive. "What else can be expected under such conditions," wrote a German priest, "than that the priceless heritage these people brought from the Fatherland gradually disappears."[14] Church authorities were very concerned about the low level of religious practice and the decline of religious fervor among the immigrants. One means they chose to remedy the situation was the national parish. No one knows how extensive the loss of faith was among German immigrants, but one thing is certain: it would have been considerably greater without the ethnic parish.

Another reason for the establishment of the national parish was the tendency of immigrants to settle in a distinct city neighborhood. By the end of the nineteenth century the majority of German-Americans lived in the city, and this pattern of settlement "put an unmistakably urban stamp upon German-American Catholicism."[16] In Philadelphia "the mid-nineteenth century was *par excellence* the era of the urban parish church."[17] It was a time when Philadelphians were creating their own island communities in a city that was slowly becoming segregated along ethnic, social, and residential lines. Philadelphia Germans were no different from their neighbors. They tended to gather together in distinctively German neighborhoods and to form their own clubs, lodges, and benefit associations. For Catholic Germans the institution that outranked all others in importance was the parish. It was not only the center of both their religious and social lives, but it also was an ethnic fortress which enabled the immigrants to resist the onslaught of the surrounding Protestant culture on their faith and tradition.

For the fifty-three years prior to 1842 there was only one German Catholic parish in Philadelphia. In the next half-century twelve more German parishes were organized.[18] As in other foreign-language groups, the laity played a prominent role in the organization of the parish. Generally they would form a society, raise the necessary money, and purchase the land for their church. They would then petition the bishop for approval of their action and request the assistance of a German-speaking priest. This pattern especially characterized the early years of development, but even in the late nineteenth century German Catholics had to take matters into their own hands if they wanted a new German parish. German Catholics accepted membership in an English-speaking parish reluctantly and only as a temporary arrangement. The Germans, like the Italians and later the Poles, were not satisfied until they had their own church. For them it was as much a cultural institution as it was a center of religion. As Catholics they desired the bishop's blessing on their work, but as Germans they would not wait for him to act. When they finished their work, the bishop had little alternative but to approve their decision.

As a link with the old country, the ethnic parish was the place where Philadelphia Germans recreated the familiar religious customs of the fatherland. According to the theologian, Catholicism was a transnational religion that knew no national distinctions. The Mass, celebrated in Latin in Irish and German parishes, was identical. The devotional life of nineteenth-century Catholicism was also strikingly similar, with special attention rendered to Jesus Christ and Mary. But the Germans, like other ethnic groups, put their own stamp on Catholic piety. They loved pageantry and pomp. They took obvious pride in elaborate ceremonies which they enthusiastically commented on in the German press. A common religion naturally exhibits similarities of expression regardless of nationality, but in those customs "not essential to Catholic faith and life" German Catholics evidenced a style of their own.[19]

Most striking was the German love of music. The parish choir was an accepted organization in any German parish, and to encourage this development Philadelphia Germans organized a city-wide Caecilien Verein in 1882.[20] Every Mass on Sunday, unlike other Catholic parishes, featured music; at the Solemn Sunday Mass an orchestra together with the choir often performed. Parish financial reports indicated that when it came to church music, money was no problem; it was generally the most costly item in the church budget.

Germans loved a parade both in and outside of church. Parish societies, outfitted in their colorful regalia and each displaying its own banner, paraded along the streets of North Philadelphia on special feast days. It was inconceivable for German Catholics to celebrate a religious festival without a colorful procession.

Spiritual confraternities were also common among German Catholics. In addition to these societies, the parish fostered the growth of mutual benefit societies. The majority of Philadelphia parishes had such *Unterstützung–Vereine*. Philadelphia Germans also belonged to the national Central Verein and in 1876 organized this society on a city-wide basis.[21] The rationale behind these benefit societies "which are found in almost every German parish" was not hard to discover.[22] They provided financial assistance in case of sickness or death; they also were a Catholic alternative to similar societies sponsored by the non-Catholic German community. The Church frowned on Catholics joining such non-Catholic vereins since they were a risk to one's "faith and eternal salvation." But a German Catholic newspaper editor argued that Catholic vereins "contribute to one's spiritual end and the good of the church."[23] Such a separatist mentality encouraged the multiplication of a panoply of parish societies for every age group. In the process it reinforced the sense of community in the parish by separating Catholics from their non-Catholic countrymen.

In addition to benefit societies, Philadelphia Germans also organized their own hospital, St. Mary's, and an orphan asylum, St. Vincent's.[24] Both institutions served the city-wide German com-

munity. Philadelphia Catholics had other hospitals and orphanages, but here too the Germans felt the need to establish
their own institutions. This was especially clear in the organization of St. Vincent's orphanage. Philadelphia had three orphan
asylums for young Catholic children when John Nepomucene
Neumann became bishop of the diocese in 1852, but these
asylums catered to the Irish and the French. Neumann saw the
need for another orphanage to care for the increasing number of
homeless German children. Benevolent institutions organized
along lines of nationality were a common feature of mid-
nineteenth-century urban Catholicism. The acute sense of
ethnicity, reinforced by the language barrier, demanded it. But
another major motivation was to save the children from
Protestantism. As Neumann put it, "asylums for our German
children are most important and most necessary. These must be
regarded as the best and only means of wresting them from the
grasp of error, of infidelity and even godlessness."[25] St.
Vincent's opened in 1855 in Tacony and eventually became a
center of German Catholicism in Northeast Philadelphia.

The fear of children losing the faith also encouraged the founding of parish schools. "By all means," urged a German guidebook, "keep your children away from the public schools which
properly ought to be called pagan schools or even worse."[26]
Equally essential was the necessity to foster the mother tongue
among the children and thus help them preserve the religious
heritage of the old country. A dilemma arose, however, because
parents also wanted their children to learn English. As a result
many parents did not heed the counsel of the clergy and sent their
children to public schools. In an attempt to counteract this
tendency German parochial schools began to use both English
and German in classroom instruction. This bilingual approach became the norm in German schools in the nineteenth century.

In Philadelphia every German parish listed in the German-
American Catholic Directory of 1892 had a school. St. Peter's,
described as "one of the most progressive city parochial
schools," was the largest German school, numbering 1,145
students; the Christian Brothers taught the boys and the School
Sisters of Notre Dame instructed the girls.[27] As was true in other
cities, however, the parochial school could never serve the

educational needs of all German children of school age. As Bishop James Wood observed in reference to the parish of St. Boniface, it was obvious "that many do not send their children to the Catholic school."[28] Given this limitation, Philadelphia Germans in particular and German Catholics in general manifested an intense commitment to parochial education. Thus, it is not surprising to discover that in 1914 over 95 percent of the German parishes in the United States had a parochial school.[29]

In building up their ethnic fortress German Catholics set themselves off from other German-Americans. In their desire to preserve their own sense of identity they "displayed fierce antagonisms against any group that infringed upon their rights."[30] Protestant Germans were a frequent object of attack. This hostile attitude was transplanted from Europe, where Protestant and Catholic Germans had been doing battle since the Reformation. "Martin Luther and his latter day followers," noted one historian, "were always the worst of heretics. In 1883, the four-hundredth anniversary of Luther's birth, the Catholic *Volkszeitung* of Baltimore, an arch-conservative paper with a national circulation, noted the occasion with a series of more than sixty articles ripping Luther, the Reformation, and Protestantism to shreds."[31] Club Germans were also objects of Catholic prejudice. Priests warned their parishioners under pain of excommunication to avoid joining such secret societies as the Freemasons, the Red Men, and the Odd Fellows, as well as the popular Turnverein.

German Catholics were also inclined to do battle among themselves. One German priest wrote that "for no other intention is there more need for prayer than for unity among the Germans—not only in the German fatherland, but also here in America."[32] The history of Holy Trinity parish, as stormy as it was, was not untypical. Factions often developed among the people causing a schism in the parish. This would result in the founding of a new parish only a few blocks away from the mother church. This was the case in Philadelphia when conflict in Holy Trinity gave birth to St. Alphonsus parish.[33] As John Hughes, the Archbishop of New York observed, German Catholics were indeed "exceedingly prone to division among themselves."[34]

The most celebrated conflict that German Catholics entered

was the struggle against the Irish-American hierarchy during the 1880s and 1890s. This was an intensely heated debate that principally involved the German communities of the Midwest triangle. The Germans of Philadelphia and Baltimore did not appear to be caught up in the issue, though this did not mean that they were unsympathetic to the cause of their Midwestern countrymen.

At the heart of the issue was the German insistence on equal rights in the American Catholic Church. This demand focused on the rights of German Catholics to have their own independent national parish where they could foster the religious heritage of the fatherland. Catholic Germans did not want to be "kept in a position inferior to that of the Irish," wrote Father Peter Abbelen of Milwaukee. "By granting the equal position which we ask," he continued," no right of the Irish would be impaired, while an injustice and a disgrace would be removed from the Germans."[35] The demand for equality for German parishes was simple enough and not a serious problem, but the hidden agenda advocated a move toward a German church independent of the Irish-American hierarchy. The Germans asked Rome to intervene on their behalf. However, the Vatican's inclination to favor the German petition and the Roman proposal to appoint a cardinal protector for German Catholics in the United States aroused the wrath of the more liberal American wing of the hierarchy. The issue was momentarily resolved in 1887, when Rome spoke out in favor of the national parish, but refused to grant further privileges to German-American Catholics.

Three years later the Lucerne Memorial rekindled the debate. The memorial was a document drawn up in Lucerne, Switzerland, in 1890 by the international representatives of the St. Raphael Verein, an immigrant aid society. The document was sent to Pope Leo XIII asking for definite rights for Catholic immigrants. In the United States it was interpreted "as another movement for German particularism." This time the demands were more comprehensive and more explicit. The goal was not just national parishes, but the development of a national clergy, national schools, and "most important of all, proportional representation in the hierarchy for each nationality."[36] The Lucerne Memorial attracted national attention in the United States. It was denounced in the Senate, and President Benjamin Harrison viewed it with concern. To both the politician and the churchman the issue was the same—the interference of foreigners in American affairs. In the 1880s and 1890s the introduction of foreign nationalism in the Catholic Church chiefly meant German nationalism, which was riding high both in the fatherland and in the United States. The reply of Rome once again favored the Americanist position, by stating that the proposals of the Lucerne Memorial were neither opportune nor necessary.

Despite the continued denial of discrimination against the Germans, they did have a legitimate complaint. Germans were not well represented in the hierarchy. In 1869 only 11 percent of the bishops were German (6 of 56). In 1900 after more than a decade of debate on the issue the proportion had increased to only 14 percent (13 of 90). The Irish had gained control of the hierarchy, and by 1900 one out of two bishops was Irish.[37] Bishops were also slow to recognize the demands of the Germans. In Philadelphia one historian observed that Bishop Wood evidenced "an unfriendly attitude toward the Germans."[38] In other cities controlled by the Irish, people complained that Church authorities "almost ignored the existence of" the Germans.[39] But it is worth noting that when the Germans gained control of the Church, as they did in Wisconsin, they began to act like the Irish in their relations with the recently arrived Polish Catholics. Fearing a German *Kulturkampf* in the Church, the Poles pushed for the same demands that Germans had fought for twenty years earlier. What was one man's cultural pluralism in the 1880s had become another person's nativism in the 1900s.[40]

What happened in Wisconsin reflected the acculturation of German-American Catholics in the years before World War I. The German language was dying out, American habits were being adopted, and the United States was becoming the fatherland for most German-Americans. Immigration of German Catholics had decreased rapidly after 1900, and the use of the German-language newspaper was also on the decline. Only three new publications appeared between 1900 and 1918.[41] In Pennsylvania the same decline was evident, and as early as 1890 "no person who taught elementary subjects in the German language was available in Pennsylvania."[42] In 1911 state law designated English as the only language of the classroom. In the parochial school the last vestige

of a commitment to the mother tongue was the use of the
German-language catechism.

The national parish was another victim of the gradual Americanization of German Catholics. In 1869 the German Catholic Directory counted 705 churches in which German was the only language used. By 1906 the number had declined to 500; ten years
later it decreased to 206. More symptomatic of the times in 1916
was the existence of 1,684 parishes in which both English and
German were used.[43]

St. Boniface parish in Philadelphia illustrated the change that
was taking place in urban America. Founded as a German parish
in 1866, it reached a population of some 1,600 families in the
1890s. In the first decade of the century the parish population declined slightly. In the next decade, according to one observer,
"many of the German people began to move north, and to the
south and west the colored people came in. At the same time, it
became clear that the younger generation did not understand
German well enough to derive any real benefit from sermons and
instructions in that language."[44]

Germans were becoming Americanized, and the old nineteenth-century settlement was breaking up as the residential patterns of twentieth-century cities shifted. Germans remained
concentrated in North Philadelphia, but the patterns of future
change were already emerging. The mother tongue was becoming
obsolete, and the nineteenth-century German parish was steadily
losing its ethnic constituency as the population of the neighborhood changed. By the end of the 1920s, writes Frederick Luebke,
"most German Catholics agreed that the goals of the church
could not be served by the preservation of German language and
culture."[45] Obviously the anti-German hysteria of World War
I hastened the process of Americanization. German-American
Catholics were disappearing as a distinctive subculture. The rise
of Adolf Hitler and the onslaught of World War II intensified
the tendency of German-Americans to bury their ethnicity. Even
though 25.5 million Americans identified themselves as individuals of German descent as recently as 1972, the group consciousness of Germans had disintegrated. Only the faintest traces
of German ethnic life remained.

In the Catholic community, people of German descent number

more than eight million, but the national parish has vanished.[46] No one clamors anymore for German bishops. The Irish are no longer the enemy. In fact, the opposite appears to be the case. If a German Catholic marries outside his group, he will most likely marry into an Irish family.[47] "If you cannot beat them, marry them" seems to be the current strategy of German-Americans.

In the nineteenth century German Catholics struggled to maintain their ethnic identity in the American Catholic Church. To a great extent they succeeded. But history was not on their side as the passage of years weakened the link with the fatherland and encouraged new allegiances to America. In 1900 the issue at stake was the persistence of German-American Catholicism. Today the question no longer is what does it mean to be a German-American Catholic, rather what does it mean to be a Catholic in America?

## Notes

1. Francis J. Herktorn, *A Retrospect of Holy Trinity Parish* (Philadelphia, 1914), pp. 6–7.
2. Ibid., p. 22.
3. These figures were calculated by Gerald Shaughnessy, *Has the Immigrant Kept the Faith?* (New York, 1925), pp.237–238, 251; and also Ernst A. Reiter, *Schematismus der katholischen deutschen Geistlichkeit* (New York, 1869), p. 232.
4. Bureau of the Census, *Religious Bodies 1916*, 2 (Washington, D.C., 1919), 654.
5. Frederick C. Luebke, *Bonds of Loyalty: German Americans and World War I* (DeKalb, Ill., 1974), p. 35.
6. Joseph Salzbacher, *Meine Reise nach Nord-Amerika im Jahre 1842* (Vienna, 1845), p. 112; Reiter, *Schematismus,* pp. 15–17; the 1892 figures are my own estimates based on data in J. N. Enzlberger, *Schematismus der katholischen Geistlichkeit deutscher Zunge in den Ver. Staaten Amerikas* (Milwaukee, 1892), pp. 232–235; *Report on Statistics of Churches in the U.S. at 11th Census 1890* (Washington, D.C., 1894), p. 245; and *Historical Sketches of the Catholic Churches and Institutions of Philadelphia* (Philadelphia, 1895), p. 18.
7. Caroline Golab, "The Immigrant and the City: Poles, Italians and Jews in Philadelphia, 1870–1920," in *The Peoples of Philadelphia,* eds. Allen F. Davis and Mark H. Haller (Philadelphia, 1973), p. 205.
8. *Berichte der Leopoldinen Stiftung,* Oct. 12, 1844, quoted by Joseph White in "German Catholics in the Diocese of Vincennes in the Nine-

teenth Century" (unpub. seminar paper, Dept. of History, University of Notre Dame, Spring 1975).

9. "Historical Studies and Notes: A Guide for Catholic German Immigrants 1869," *Social Justice Review*, 52 (July–Aug. 1959), 135.

10. John M. Lenhart, O.F.M., "Historical Studies and Notes: Statistical Accounts of Membership of German Catholics in America," *Social Justice Review*, 51 (Jan. 1959), 312.

11. Jay P. Dolan, *The Immigrant Church: New York's Irish and German Catholics, 1815–1865* (Baltimore, 1975), p. 71.

12. John M. Lenhart, O.F.M., "Historical Studies and Notes: German Catholics in the Diocese of Philadelphia in 1846," *Central-Blatt and Social Justice*, 26 (July–Aug. 1933), 131.

13. *Historical Sketches of the Catholic Churches*, p. 73.

14. Michael J. Curley, C.SS.R., *Venerable John Neumann* (New York, 1952), pp. 222–223.

15. Quoted in Dolan, *Immigrant Church*, pp. 84–85.

16. Luebke, *Bonds of Loyalty*, p. 36.

17. Sam Bass Warner Jr., *The Private City* (Philadelphia, 1971), p. 61.

18. Enzlberger, *Schematismus*, pp. 232–235.

19. Dolan, *The Immigrant Church*, pp. 79–80.

20. Enzlberger, *Schematismus*, p. 325.

21. Ibid., p. 324; these parish societies are listed in *Historical Sketches of the Catholic Churches*, pp. lvii–lviii.

22. "Historical Studies and Notes: A Guide," p. 166.

23. Ibid.; *Katholische Kirchenzeitung*, Sept. 2, 1858.

24. Enzlberger, *Schematismus*, p. 181.

25. Curley, *Venerable John Neumann*, pp. 260–261; see also Francis X. Roth, *History of St. Vincent's Orphan Asylum, Tacony, Philadelphia* (Philadelphia, 1934). On the German Catholics' unhappy experience in public hospitals which led to the establishment of German hospitals see Archives of the Archdiocese of New York, Claims of the Fathers and the Congregation of the Church of the Most Holy Redeemer, New York, to St. Francis Hospital, Fifth Street, New York, July 20, 1868.

26. "Historical Studies and Notes: A Guide," p. 167.

27. Enzlberger, *Schematismus*, pp. 232–235; Thomas J. Donaghy, *Philadelphia's Finest: A History of Education in the Catholic Archdiocese 1692–1970* (Philadelphia, 1972), p. 88.

28. John F. Byrne, C.SS.R., *The Redemptorist Centenaries* (Philadelphia, 1932), p. 193.

29. Richard M. Linkh, *American Catholicism and European Immigrants* (Staten Island, N.Y., 1975), p. 110.

30. Luebke, *Bonds of Loyalty*, p. 36.

31. Ibid., p. 37.

32. Quoted by Sister M. Mileta Ludwig, F.S.P.A., "Sources for the Biography of Michael Heiss, Bishop of LaCrosse, 1868–1880 and Archbishop of Milwaukee, 1881–1890," *Records* of the American Catholic Historical Society of Philadelphia, 79 (Dec. 1968), 210.

33. Curley, *Venerable John Neumann*, pp. 222–224.

34. Archives of the University of Notre Dame, *Scritture Riferite nei Congressi; American Centrale*, vol. 18, letter 1417, John Hughes to Prefect of Propaganda Fide, Mar. 23, 1858, f. 511.

35. Colman J. Barry, *The Catholic Church and German Americans* (Milwaukee, 1953), p. 291.

36. Colman J. Barry, "The German Catholic Immigrant," in *Roman Catholicism and the American Way of Life*, ed., Thomas T. McAvoy (Notre Dame, 1960), p. 199.

37. These figures were calculated from Reiter, *Schematismus*, p. 232 and p. 234; the list of German clergy compiled in Enzlberger, *Schematismus*, pp. 352–381; Bernard J. Code, *Dictionary of the American Hierarchy* (New York, 1940); and the *U.S. Catholic Directory 1900*.

38. Michael J. Curley, C.SS.R., *The Provincial Story* (New York, 1963), p. 161.

39. Dolan, *Immigrant Church*, p. 72.

40. Anthony J. Kuzniewski Jr., "Faith and Fatherland: An Intellectual History of the Polish Immigrant Community in Wisconsin, 1838–1918" (unpub. doctoral dissertation, Harvard University, 1973).

41. Philip Gleason, *The Conservative Reformers* (Notre Dame, 1968), p. 48.

42. Homer Tope Rosenberger, *The Pennsylvania Germans 1891–1965* (Lancaster, 1966), pp. 70–71.

43. Reiter, *Schematismus*, p. 232; Linkh, *American Catholicism*, pp. 108–110.

44. Byrne, *The Redemptorist Centenaries*, p. 188.

45. Luebke, *Bonds of Loyalty*, p. 317.

46. Harold J. Abramson, *Ethnic Diversity in Catholic America* (New York, 1973), p. 19.

47. Ibid., pp. 51–67.

Chapter 5

# Faith and Fatherland
## Dimensions of Polish-American Ethnoreligion, 1875–1975

William J. Galush

In 1887 Victor Zaleski and Jan Radziejewski founded a newspaper in Chicago; they called it *Wiara i Ojczyzna* (Faith and Fatherland).[1] The title of this early Roman Catholic periodical aptly summarized the dominant attitude about the nature of Polishness *(Polskość)*: that Roman Catholicism and national identity were inseparably linked. While a secularist concept of Polishness was present on both sides of the ocean, a majority in America and the homeland gave a religious dimension to their ethnicity.[2]

Given this general commitment to a traditional faith, the relationship of religion to ethnicity requires some definition. Harry S. Stout has argued persuasively that these factors may properly be treated as identical by scholars in the sense that they express the same phenomenon. Stout cites Milton M. Gordon's definition of ethnicity as "a network of organizations and informal social relationships which permits and encourages the members of the ethnic group to remain within the confines of the group for all of their primary relationships and some of their secondary relationships throughout all stages of the life cycle."[3] Beside this may be set Stout's concept of religion as "the commonly shared personal perception of ultimate allegiance that supplies coherence and community on a group level." Most importantly, it is "in this context that personal religious allegiance and socio-cultural expression interact and reinforce one another."[4] This ethnoreligion is not static; rather, it develops in a three-stage typology first suggested by Will Herberg. The first is the immigrant phase, limited to specific national origins and church forms. Next comes a merging into a broader grouping of Protestant-Catholic-Jew and finally the most inclusive stage of a national religion of the "American way of life."[5] Different groups are in different stages in this approximate grouping, with only the first and second now evident. To conceive of Poles in the United States as developing within this typology will be helpful in our examination of Polonian* ethnoreligion over the last century. Since the subjective aspects of religiosity, such as piety and commitment, are very difficult to measure, the discussion will concentrate on the interaction of Poles with their religious institutions in Poland and America.

In the partitioned homeland of the nineteenth century the faith served ethnicity in several ways. It distinguished Poles from Protestant Prussians and Orthodox Russians and other Slavs, and it was also the one institution which transcended partition boundaries. Although the Catholic hierarchy usually remained politically passive, many priests sometimes offered local patriotic as well as spiritual leadership.[6] This was especially important since the vast majority of the population were ill-educated peasants whose nationalism was undeveloped in comparison with their local *(okolica)* orientation.[7] Unlike their Russian counterparts, Polish peasants were seldom drawn to religious heterodoxy.[8] This orthodoxy fostered a general obedience to priests and bishops.

Practices were more familiar than dogmas to the persons who made up the bulk of immigrants, and some items in their "cultural baggage" were to cause controversy in the New World environment. One was a familiarity with lay intervention in church affairs. Most obvious was the *ius patronatus,* the right of patronage by which a local noble might nominate a pastor to a parish which his ancestors had endowed.[9] While the parishioners were unable

*"Polonia" refers to a concentration of Poles outside the homeland, either local or national as the context suggests.

to participate formally in this process—though they might informally make their preferences known—its very existence accustomed them to a significant lay role in church affairs. In
America a democratization of the patron concept, coupled with
other factors, led to a serious schism among Poles.

The half-century before World War I saw an ever-increasing
stream of Polish immigrants, first from German Poland and then
from Russian and Austrian Poland. This concentration produced
American Polonia, which by 1914 numbered between two and
four million persons, mainly young and middle-aged, and most
born in the fatherland.[10] They came seeking a more prosperous
life and also freedom from religious and cultural oppression. They
found both a modest prosperity and a gratifying absence of
governmental interference.[11]

Their religious experience in America was mixed. Poles encountered an established Roman Catholic Church into which they
had to fit. This largest of American denominations, growing
rapidly and imperfectly organized, seemed to be under the control of an earlier ethnic group, the Irish. Persons from the Emer-
ald Isle had formed the first large Catholic immigration, and after
1850 Irish-Americans dominated the fast-growing American
hierarchy.[12] Yet to say that predominance of one ethnic group
among the bishops represented a triumph for one ethnicity over
another is misleading. As students of the Irish in America have
demonstrated, bishops of Hibernian ancestry could be indifferent
or even hostile to Irish-American aspirations and causes.[13] The
episcopate had more concern for control than for Parnell, more
worry about its authority than about the Ascendancy. In denominational affairs this may be seen most clearly in the early and
persistent struggle against "trusteeism." In the absence of effective episcopal supervision, laymen often founded and administered congregations, even hiring and discharging priests. These
practices found increasing disfavor with bishops intent upon es-
tablishing their authority.[14] A series of sharp battles culminated
in the decrees of the first Provincial Synod of Baltimore in 1829,
which forbade parishioners to hold the church property and
denied any alleged rights to administer the parish or nominate its
pastor.[15] By the time Poles arrived in significant numbers much
later in the century, these questions were settled, and the Irish-
descended laity were accustomed to the post-1829 order.

In another important area, however, the hierarchy made a concession to ethnicity. This was the national parish, countenanced by the bishops initially to placate German Catholics unhappy with Irish-dominated territorial parishes. Although an expedient rather than a norm, ethnically enclosed congregations defused potential explosions at the critical local level.[16] In light of the immigrant tendency to identify religion with ethnicity, the absence of such a policy would have produced greater turbulence and perhaps several schisms.

Poles brought with them a religion steeled by adversity, a symbol of resistance to the partitioning powers. Special feast days, hymns, and other customs provided a rich religious heritage, and in America the parish took on perhaps even more meaning than at home. The congregation in the United States was not given; rather, it was the recent and conscious creation of laymen and clerics determined to re-establish the central village institution in the strange and sometimes frightening new land. Of necessity lay persons played a major, even dominant role in parish formation. An absence of Polish priests, the presence of lay voluntary associations led by ambitious and religious men, and a felt need for an ethnically enclosed place of worship led to the establishment of congregations in settlements shortly after a more specialized and limited group form—usually fraternal aid societies—arose.

The process may be seen well in Cleveland. In the early 1890s Poles began to concentrate in the near South Side, far from ethnic parishes on the east side of the Cuyahoga River. By 1898 a committee formed under the leadership of a society officer, Joseph Kmiecik, and petitioned Bishop Ignatius F. Horstmann for a parish and pastor. Such petitions were an effective cue to ordinaries with otherwise spotty information on ethnic concentrations and desires, and in this instance the reply was affirmative:

I sent for Father Benedict Rosinski [pastor of St. Stanislaus parish on the East Side] for information concerning your petition for a Polish school and church on the South Side. We agreed at once that it was necessary. I asked him to organize the congregation and hope to be able to obtain a priest in time to take charge. Of course the Poles must subscribe at once to pay for the ground, but let them be careful not to speak of it. When the neighborhood is fixed, I will get someone to purchase the ground.[17]

The reply demonstrates several aspects of a prudent bishop's policy in handling such requests. Bishop Horstmann quickly consulted a knowledgeable and trustworthy outsider and then hastened to insert the priest into the process of congregational formation. This not only provided the laymen with experienced clerical leadership, but also assured the bishop that further effort would develop under priestly direction. Likewise, the use of an episcopal agent to purchase land with Polish money on the pretext of a lower price served a covert purpose, since immigrant enthusiasm would have made this one of the worst-kept secrets on the South Side. By this means Horstmann secured title to the property directly and immediately, thus avoiding having to seek explicit permission from the Polish donors. Kmiecik and his fellow committeemen may have been aware of these tactics, but their overwhelming desire to erect an ethnic congregation overrode any reluctance.

Though overseen by clerics, the formation of what became St. John Cantius parish began by lay initiative and was sustained by elected lay leaders and voluntary support from the immigrants as a whole. Since a congregation was also a civil corporation, this posed further problems for episcopal authority. The solution here as elsewhere was to control as much as possible the choice of officers, who always included some laymen.[18] In this instance, Horstmann ordered the new pastor, Father Hipolyt Orlowski, to "appoint four reliable councilors" to a parish committee *(komitet parafialny)* to help administer the congregation.[19] Perhaps to avoid conflict with his proud flock, Orlowski instead permitted their nomination and election at an annual all-parish meeting, a procedure familiar to the laity from older local voluntary associations and used in the choice of the original parish committee. Such tampering with the system finally earned the priest a rebuke in 1903:

Your people must learn to recognize that the statutes of the diocese must be observed by them just the same as they are by every other congregation in the diocese.

In voting for councilmen it is the exclusive right of the pastor to present the names of those who can be voted for. If the voters disobey that law, the Bishop then appoints the councilmen.

Bishop Horstmann ended his admonition with a significant question: "Why is it that only the Poles cause trouble in this regard?"[20]

National parishes emerged in an atmosphere of lay initiative and democratic participation, and immigrants sought to legitimize a continued lay role in congregational affairs via committees well into the interwar era. Popular concern with the parish was so intense that it suggests a qualification to the first stage of Stout's typology of religious development. There seems in early Polonia to have been a focus even narrower than immigrant religion, which may be termed "localism." This was a New World equivalent of an *okolica* (rural district) orientation, with the center here being the new parish created with so much effort. The masses of laity perceived issues much more sharply on the congregational level. In turn, this affected such topics as religious dissent and pressure for Polish-American bishops.

The appearance of widespread, if minority, dissent depended on a variety of factors, not least of which was the character and image of the local pastor. From the immigrant priest's perspective, a pastorate in the United States offered both advantages and disadvantages. The advantages included government indifference and the necessary reliance of a non-Polish-speaking bishop on his Polish priests for regular information on a parish. This comparative lack of episcopal oversight had its counterpart in the absence of high status laymen with traditional prerogatives in nomination and administration. The typical immigrant was of peasant background and came with habits of deference congenial to old-country priests. On the other hand, greater lay involvement in parish affairs and priestly interests in the preservation of traditional ethnicity made conflict possible and even likely in numerous areas. An interesting result was the formation by 1900 of a number of clerical societies to give Polish priests greater influence in dealing with laity and bishops alike.[21] The central position of the pastor inevitably involved him in a parish quarrel, and often he was at the center of it.

The circumstances of immigrant existence favored the emergence of strong lay leaders, men who might never had had much impact on their villages at home. In the urban residential concentrations amidst a larger and indifferent society a common ethnic background fostered a casual sense of community. Various impulses moved immigrants toward a more purposeful development of group consciousness, influenced by common religious, cultural, and political aspirations and a practical need for united effort against adversity. The most important form of voluntary association to develop was the fraternal aid society. Modeled on those of older ethnic groups, these lodges offered numerous posts for ambitious men. Election and advancement required persuasiveness, native intelligence, and administrative ability. Once established, leaders often held high office in several societies, either simultaneously or serially, demonstrating by continued reelection their high status in the community.[22] If they were not vociferous anti-clericals, such men might assume parish posts as well. Their previous experience bred self-confidence and a sense of democratic form and responsibility, which in certain circumstances might not fit Bishop Horstmann's definition of "reliable."

In addition to the rise of prominent laymen there was also the factor of a developing Polish nationalism. From an early date editors and organization leaders sought to nurture a group consciousness transcending locality.[23] A visiting Galician intellectual noted approvingly in 1894 that "here for the first time we meet Poles from all areas of partitioned Poland in one common territory—here the Polish spirit is most powerfully propagated."[24] In competition with secular nationalists, Polish Roman Catholics insisted that they did "not comprehend patriotism without God and faith."[25] This attitude, captured in the slogan *Bóg i Ojczyzna* (God and Fatherland), contained no disloyalty to the Roman Catholic Church. Yet persons dissatisfied with American Catholicism might take this religio-nationalism and apply it to a specifically Polish form of Catholicism, asserting a superior purity unmarred by "foreign" elements.

During the 1890s religious dissent appeared in many Polish colonies. While initially local, some independent congregations coalesced into small denominations by 1900. The earliest such sects were led by former Roman Catholic priests, Anton Kozlowski of Chicago and Stephan Kaminski of Buffalo, but the most successful and enduring emerged under Francis Hodur of Scranton, Pennsylvania. Father Hodur, an immigrant Galician priest, became the spiritual leader of a group of strong-willed and dissatisfied laymen from Sacred Heart Church in Scranton in 1897. The dissenters demanded three administrative changes from established Roman Catholic polity: congregational ownership of church property and a lay role in the adminstration and in the selection of priests.[26] These demands conflicted with the decrees of the Synod of 1829, and Bishop Michael J. Hoban, following similar episcopal practice elsewhere, refused to grant them. His refusal provided Hodur and lay leaders a basis for attacking the hierarchy as undemocratic.[27]

At least as important as polity was personality. The unhappy laymen sitgmatized their former pastor, Father Richard Aust, as tyrannical and arbitrary. Such allegations vied in popularity with charges of clerical immorality and episcopal dictatorship and provided a living focus for resentment, and for defense as well.[28]

Despite the vituperation and occasional violence which accompanied these schisms, a doctrinal and ritual conservatism marked all the movements. While retaining most Roman Catholic beliefs and customs in the context of a democratized parish and denominational polity, Hodur's Polish National Catholic Church stressed a mystical and specific ethnoreligiosity:

Should we disinherit our souls, and deprive ourselves of independence, in order that we might please the Pope and the Irish bishops? No, never! If our nation has any mission in humanity's research for higher goals, then it must also have its own distinct Polish faith, its national church, as all creative peoples of the world have.''[29]

Although promoted diligently in a powerful rhetoric, less than 5 percent of Polish immigrants joined the National Catholics before 1914, and this proportion would seem to be true in later years as well.[30] Reluctance to leave the Roman Catholic Church does not lend itself to documentation, but likely subjective elements include inertia, fear of minority status, family influences, and unwillingness to leave a congregation which one had helped build.

While the national parish environment engaged the interest of the average layman, the possibility of Polish-American bishops drew the attention of many clerics and some lay leaders. As early as 1886 a Father Ignatius Barzcz wrote from his New Jersey pastorate to Bishop Richard Gilmour of Cleveland to solicit his support for a Polish bishop as Gilmour's suffragan.[31] In the early 1890s Polish Catholic leaders supported Peter Paul Cahensly's call for ethnic hierarchies, but their still modest numbers had little effect.[32] Episcopal hostility was so intimidating that Poles never tried to imitate the German example even when their numbers and organization were greater.

Instead, the main thrust of Polish-American effort went toward getting bishops in territorial dioceses. Newspaper editorials and clerical lobbying were common tactics, but the immigrant generality never became aroused to the level of demonstration and petition that accompanied local parish quarrels.[33] The results were disappointing. By the First World War only two persons of Polish background, Paul P. Rhode and Edward Kozlowski, had been consecrated bishops. Their proportion in the hierarchy was far less than the 10 percent of the general Catholic population composed of Poles.[34] This tiny representation suggested discrimination, but another factor was the episcopal fear that Poles, like the other non-Irish churchmen, might support ethnicity and even separate episcopates.[35] To return to the typology, the native-born bishops aspired to the second stage of ethnoreligion, a general and post-immigrant Catholicism, and bishops with strong ethnic ties might impede progress toward that goal.

In contrast to the rather distant aim of Polish-American bishops, a cause which affected laymen directly might transcend parish lines. One such issue was a Polish cemetery for Philadelphia. Poles traditionally wished to be laid to rest among their compatriots, and in 1912 a local newspaper, *Patryota* (Patriot), noted that a parish in Nicetown had bought land for this purpose some time before and now wished to develop it for use. The obstacle had been and was the archbishop. Archbishop Patrick J. Ryan did not approve it in his day and his successor, Edmund F. Prendergast, continued this refusal. The editor asserted that the archbishops wished to encourage the use of diocesan cemeteries but stigmatized these as "German-Irish."[36] A few weeks later *Patryota* commented approvingly on a mass meeting at St. Adalbert's parish to arouse support for the new cemetery and noted that others had been held or were scheduled. The editor expressed the hope that "the archbishop may hear and acknowledge the demands of the Poles if he sees that we are united and working together for a desired goal."[37] *Patryota* stressed both an obligation of ethnic solidarity and the advantages of impressing non-Poles with Polish unity. The issue had become laden with more than the overt purpose of securing a cemetery; it was to help create a supra-parish consciousness and perhaps to diminish non-Polish opposition on future issues.

Congregational and community affairs affected the immigrant generation; education determined succeeding ones. The parish school was to be the transmitter of Polishness. This reflected a consensus reached among Polonian Catholic leaders by 1900 on the ineffectiveness of parental instruction.[38] As the editor of Minneapolis' *Słońce* (Sun) declared in that year,   parents "work and do not have the time to give a Polish and religious education to their children."[39] Thus Polish priests and lay leaders committed their followers to heavy expenditures for schools and staff, and the immigrant generality responded generously. The parishes of Philadelphia were typical; all built schools within five years of their foundation.[40] The original instructors were often organists from the old country, but teaching sisters rapidly replaced them. Although inadequate in numbers and with less pedagogical preparation than their public school counterparts, Polish and mixed congregations made heroic efforts to service the multiplying schools. By 1912 there were some 350.[41]

American bishops watched this spread of Polish elementary education with approval. In comparison with Italians or even Slovaks, Poles set up schools in greater proportion.[42] This approval concealed a difference in educational intent. The immigrants saw their schools as nurturing a religion of a specific ethnic group; the bishops ideally wanted to foster a post-ethnic Catholicism. Expediency and prudence stilled episcopal criticism before World War I, but during and after the conflict the attitude of the hierarchy changed to the detriment of Polonian aspirations.

Though sometimes illiterate, the immigrants had a fervent desire to see their children receive at least an elementary education, and most Catholics sent their offspring to parochial school for at least a few years.[43] From the start the schools had some English instruction, perhaps more than one-half by the eve of the war, with Polish used in religion, history, literature, and the language itself.[44] For them this was not a betrayal of ethnicity; rather, it was an affirmation of their commitment to America and a conscious realization that competence in English was necessary for success in the United States. The willingness of the immigrant generality to view Polish instruction unsentimentally may have provoked grim forbodings in perceptive leaders devoted to the indefinite preservation of Polish culture. The postwar era in fact saw significant changes.

The advent of European war shocked and engrossed American Polonia. The immigrants wept at the carnage wrought by battle in their homeland, but in the strife saw hope for the resurrection of Poland. To coordinate relief and propaganda efforts and eventually military recruiting, Catholic leaders formed the National Department (Wydział Narodowy).[45] Parishes were the local centers, and the cause of liberated Poland took on the character of a crusade. The departure of recruits for training was a moment of high emotion and an occasion for expressing solidarity in an ethnoreligious setting.[46] The war had a broadening effect on Poles, moving some out of their localities as soldiers and interesting more in concerns which transcended the parish.

Jubilation at victory gradually gave way to unanticipated tensions in Polonia. There was universal satisfaction at the rebirth of Poland, but certain trends in the new state caused increasing concern and irritation. Polonians met successive appeals for loans and gifts to the new state with generosity, but requests for donations to the numerous political parties became insupportable during the early twenties. This reaction was not a rejection of ties with Poland; rather, American Poles wished to dissociate themselves from politics with little relevance but great capacity for agitation. The Union of Polish Priests (Zjednoczenie Kapłanów Polskich), meeting in 1922, was perhaps the first organization to break openly with the previous preoccupation with Polish homeland issues. Led by Bishop Paul P. Rhode, the assembled clergy discussed only domestic concerns: the need for more Polonian bishops, the role of Polish-American priests in the National Catholic Welfare Conference, relations with other organizations, and social and labor questions.[47] A few months later Rhode met with other Catholic organization heads to prepare an agenda for the upcoming Emigration Congress, composed of delegates from all the major Catholic and most non-socialist societies. The items approved dealt exclusively with Polonia. There were five major points, most of which have persisted to the present in some form. They were maintenance of the Polish language in parish schools, combatting attacks by Americanization extremists, more Polonian bishops, enrolling youth in Polish-American organizations, and the fostering of the Polish spirit in the second generation.[48] With the partial exception of World War II and its aftermath, the fundamental shift in emphasis toward domestic concerns has never been altered.

A modification of this list will comprise the remaining topics to be considered in this chapter. Excesses in Americanization may be excluded as a transient issue, and the desire for more bishops has been partially satisfied over the years.[49] More essential to this inquiry are the remaining items, which may be rephrased as the extent and nature of Polishness in parochial education and the persistence of an ethnic orientation in the post-immigrant generations.

In terms of formal education, the interwar period might seem to be the golden age of Polonia. Polish Roman Catholic grade schools exceeded 500 by 1927, served by more nuns in better equipped buildings than ever before.[50] Yet amidst these improvements both foreign and domestic observers agreed that the Polish elements of instruction were diminishing, which was a cause for concern to ethnic leaders sincerely committed to Polishness and dependent on its continued existence for much of their status. These priests and laymen had for several decades vigorously supported formal instruction in Polish language, culture, and religion as essential to group identity, and yet their combined efforts could not halt what they clearly regarded as unwelcome change. Numerous factors seem to have contributed to this trend, with their cumulative effect being irresistible in the long run.

Episcopal attitudes became more hostile toward foreign-language instruction during and after World War I. The ethnic press was filled with articles condemning new diocesan regulations which curtailed or forbade the use of non-English school materials. Although the bishops did not always enforce these rules, their very existence antagonized the Poles.[51] While this opposition may have declined in recent years because of increased interest in cultural pluralism, such toleration has come rather late to aid Polishness.

Another external pressure was state law. Requirements mandated by state school commissions could affect non-public schools. During the Red Scare of 1919, some fifteen states passed laws requiring all instruction in public and private schools to be in English.[52] Even without such hysterical attacks on "foreignism," the specification of increasing numbers of subjects by the states cut down on the time available for Polish-language instruction.[53]

Conceivably the parish schools might have ignored or accommodated to these external pressures and still maintained a significant Polish curriculum, but internal changes diluted the will to do so. Developments in teaching personnel were part of this. While the original nuns had almost always been immigrants, they eagerly sought recruits among girls born here. Simultaneously they reacted to parental and internal pressures for superior pedagogical training. The result by the interwar period was a growing proportion of American-born sisters with better academic preparation and a weaker knowledge of and interest in Polish culture.[54] Ethnic congregations came more and more to resemble their mixed equivalents, and in the absence of large influxes of nuns from Poland this trend has continued to the present.

Most parents went along with the dimunition of Polish subjects. Although loyal in their own minds to church and ancestry, immigrants wanted their children to be as well-prepared as possible to compete in the American marketplace. They also may have been less interested in immigrant religion by the interwar era, as the following pattern suggests. In both a Cleveland and a Minneapolis parish during this time about one quarter of the pupils entered parochial school about the second grade and left after the fifth or sixth. This coincided with first holy communion or confirmation.[55] A pattern of departure after a major ritual event hinted at more interest in a general Catholicism than concern for extended instruction in Polishness.

The youngsters probably affected Polish school curriculums, but this also requires inference. Even before World War I the ethnic press editorialized against the alleged tendency of youth to converse in English instead of Polish.[56] For the second generation, however, speaking English made sense. English was the language of the streets and of general society, and parents seem to have often accepted it at home among the children.[57] The students' weak acquaintance with and obvious disinterest in Polish linguistic and cultural studies hardly discouraged nuns lacking strong Polish backgrounds from moving toward an all-English curriculum.

The overall effect of these factors in the national parish schools was to dilute the ethnic content of instruction, which largely disappeared after World War II. But if an inculcation of Polish culture diminished or disappeared, a commitment in both the second and third generations to religious education remained strong. While the statistics are not strictly comparable, my research in three different cities showed that 78 percent of a second-generation sample had at least some parochial schooling. In a nation-wide study in 1966, Andrew M. Greeley and Peter H. Rossi found that children of "Polish" extraction (presumably third or even fourth generation) in a national sample had a rate of 73 percent.[58]

Several important changes occured in congregational life as well. A noticeable decline in controversy within parish committees typified those I have studied in the interwar period.[59] While the formation of Polish National Catholic congregations may have removed the most vocal dissenters, the lessening of conflict perhaps had more to do with second–generation acceptance of the authoritarian American Catholic parish polity. With no memories of traditions of lay intervention to stir them to fight for alleged rights, the maturing offspring of the immigrants could have a quieting effect. The pattern of independent church formation offers some support to this assertion. The third decade, 1917–1926, of the Polish National Catholic Church saw its greatest growth in terms of new congregations, and the rate declined steadily and ever more sharply thereafter, simultaneous with the achievement of adulthood of vast numbers of second-generation Polish-Americans.[60] Probably contributing significantly to this peaceful trend were the new American-born Roman Catholic priests of Polish parentage. They appeared by World War I, using native English and accustomed to American social informality. Some of them joined the business and social clubs of upwardly mobile second-generation persons and socialized on

equal terms with well-educated and increasingly affluent Polonians in a manner unheard of in the immigrant generation.[61]

The exodus from the original parishes, noticeable before World
War II and accelerated after, had negative effects on immigrant
religion. The policy of the bishops had long been to make it easy
to leave ethnic parishes, and affluent young people sought better
homes elsewhere, often in areas without any Polish parishes.[62]
Part of this mobility was not economic; it reflected increasing
intermarriage as well. In two parishes in Cleveland and Minneapolis, the rate of endogamy from 1920 to 1940 slipped from 95
percent to 75 percent and 78 percent to 44 percent respectively.[63]
Recent figures show a continuing tendency toward intermarriage
in the third generation as well.[64] Given the decreasing availability
of spouses in parishes with shrinking populations, as well as a
lessening ethnic orientation, this increase in exogamy is not
surprising. It should be noted, however, that Poles of the third
generation show the same strong inclination to be members of the
Church, so that aspect of religiosity has been retained.[65]

The tendency of religion among Poles in America has been in
the direction of the second stage of ethnoreligion. The impressive
immigrant effort which established hundreds of national parishes
provided a center for a vigorous Polishness before World War I.
Immigrant religiosity clashed with American episcopal policies,
but in spite of minor schisms the bulk of Polish immigrants
remained loyal to the Roman Catholic Church. Vast expenditures
of money and personnel were aimed at transmitting Polishness to
the children through parochial education, but several factors
severely limited its ethnic effectiveness. The second and subsequent generations developed more as Catholics of Polish
descent than as Polish Catholics, although their strong attachment to Church membership may be termed an ethnic characteristic. This would seem to be the Polish heritage in America:
loyalty to a general Roman Catholicism with a lingering commitment to immigrant religious forms embodied in the national
parishes.

## Notes

1. Jan Wepsiec, *Polish American Serial Publications 1842–1966: An
Annotated Bibliography* (Chicago, 1968), p. 164.

2. E.g., Oscar Halecki, *A History of Poland* (New York, 1943), pp. 12–13 and 257–258; for a grudging affirmation by Marxist writers see, for example, Aleksander Gieysztor, *History of Poland* (Warsaw, 1968), pp.58–59 and 533–536.

3. Milton M. Gordon, "Assimilation in American Theory and Reality," *Daedalus,* 90 (Spring, 1961), 280.

4. Harry H. Stout, "Ethnicity: The Vital Center of Religion in America," *Ethnicity,* 2 (June 1975), 206.

5. Ibid., pp. 207–208; cf. also Will Herberg, *Protestant-Catholic-Jew* (Garden City, New York, 1960).

6. Stefan Kieniewicz, *The Emancipation of the Polish Peasantry* (Chicago, 1969), p. 195; and Antoni Gurnicz, *Kółka rolnicze w Galicji* (Warsaw, 1967), pp. 60 and 78–80.

7. William I. Thomas and Florian Znaniecki, *The Polish Peasant in Europe and America,* 1 (New York, rprt. 1958), 143–144.

8. Ibid., p. 287.

9. Cf. *Polak w Ameryce* (Buffalo), Mar. 4, 1897; and *Kuryer Polski* (Milwaukee), Sept. 26, 1913, for descriptions and criticisms of this homeland practice.

10. Precise statistics on immigration are not yet available (and are probably unobtainable), but useful articles are Victor R. Greene; "Pre-World War I Polish Emigration to the United States: Motives and Statistics," *Polish Review,* 6 (Summer, 1961), 46–67; and Jerzy Zubrzycki, "Emigration from Poland in the Nineteenth and Twentieth Centuries," *Population Studies,* 6 (Mar. 1953), 248–272.

11. William J. Galush, "Forming Polonia: A Study of Four Polish-American Communities, 1890–1940" (unpub. doctoral dissertation, University of Minnesota, 1975), pp. 115 and 267 for statistics on occupational mobility among sample Poles in Minneapolis, Cleveland, and Utica. A fine example of Polish appreciation of American civil liberty may be found in Stanisław Osada. *Historya Związka Narodowego Polskiego,* 1 (Chicago, rprt. 1957), 123.

12. Thomas T. McAvoy, *A History of the Catholic Church in the United States* (Notre Dame, 1969), pp. 163–166.

13. Cf. Thomas N. Brown, *Irish-American Nationalism 1870–1890* (Philadelphia, 1966), pp. 148–150, and Donna Merwick, *Boston's Priests, 1848–1910: A Study of Social and Intellectual Change* (Cambridge, Mass., 1973), pp. 116–123.

14. McAvoy, *A History of the Catholic Church,* pp. 92–122, and Theodore Maynard, *The Story of American Catholicism* (New York, 1960), pp. 173–186.

15. Patrick J. Dignan, *A History of the Legal Incorporation of*

*Catholic Church Property in the United States, 1784–1932* (Washington, D.C., 1933), pp. 145–146.

16. Vincent J. Fecher, *A Study of the Movement for German National Parishes in Philadelphia and Baltimore, 1787–1802* (Rome, 1955). A recent work by Victor R. Greene, *For God and Country: The Rise of Polish and Lithuanian Ethnic Consciousness in America, 1860–1910* (Madison, Wisc., 1975), takes up many of the points discussed in this chapter. I found his division of Poles concerned with fostering ethnic consciousness into "religionists" (Roman Catholics) and "nationalists" (a more secularist orientation) acceptable. Their competition certainly did force a growth of ethnic consciousness.

While in basic agreement with this, I have a differing interpretation of similar data on several important points which lack of space prevents me from treating in sufficient detail. First, I have found no significant difference in "patriotism" between the two camps. Innumerable Roman Catholic-sponsored rallies and editorials in the Catholic press spoke of the need for Polish independence, although in the context of linking Catholicism with true Polishness. Second, Greene gives insufficient attention to the attraction of democracy in his interpretation of parish quarrels. Poles came to America with long acquaintance with lay interference in church affairs by the state and local nobles. The homeland *ius patronatus* (right of patronage) was democratized in America by a laity which typically took the initiative in congregation formation. Habits of lay independence led to conflict with clergy and bishops, not to mention personality and other idiosyncratic factors. Finally, I would emphasize the importance of localism. Greene tends to project the Chicago experience, with its bevy of articulate and ideologically sophisticated leaders, upon all Polonia. Conflict between "religionists" and "nationalists" depended much more on the local situation than on official ideological affiliation, as I found in Minneapolis, Cleveland, and Utica. Cf. Galush, "Forming Polonia."

17. Horstmann to Kmiecik, Mar. 21, 1898, St. John Cantius File, Archives of the Diocese of Cleveland (henceforth ADC).

18. Dignan's *A History of the Legal Incorporation* gives an extended analysis of state laws and episcopal responses.

19. Horstmann to Orlowski, Dec. 23, 1898, St. John Cantius File, ADC.

20. Horstmann to Orlowski, Jan. 24, 1903, St. John Cantius File, ADC.

21. Galush, "Forming Polonia," p. 53.

22. Ibid., pp. 151–154 for a study of officeholding patterns in ethnic societies in Utica, New York.

23. Osada, *Historya*, p. 123; *Zgoda* (Chicago), July 14, 1898; for at-

tacks on regional and partitional loyalties see *Kuryer Polski,* Feb. 7, 1915.

24. *Przegląd Emigracyjny* (Cracow), Jan. 1, 1894.

25. *Polak w Ameryce,* Jan. 14, 1897.

26. *Po drodze życia w 25-tą rocznicę powstania Polskiego Narodowego Kościoła* (Scranton, 1922), p. 15. For a Roman Catholic orientation on this episode see John P. Gallagher, *A Century of History: The Diocese of Scranton, 1868–1968* (Scranton, 1968), p. 223 and pass.

27. William J. Galush, "The Polish National Catholic Church: A Survey of Its Origins, Development and Missions," *Records* of the American Catholic Historical Society of Philadelphia, 83 (Sept.–Dec. 1972), 131–149.

28. Ibid., pp. 140–142; and *Jutrzenka* (Cleveland), Apr. 11, 1894.

29. *Księga pamiątkowa "33"* (Scranton, 1930), pp. 88–89.

30. Galush, "The Polish National Catholic Church," pp. 148–149.

31. Barzcz to Gilmour, Apr. 8, 1886, ADC.

32. Robert D. Cross, *The Rise of Liberal Catholicism* (Cambridge, Mass. 1958), pp. 92–93; and McAvoy, *History of the Catholic Church,* pp. 292 and 295–296.

33. E.g., *Wiarus* (Winona, Minn.), Feb. 15, 1906. For episcopal hostility see James H. Moynihan, *The Life of Archbishop John Ireland* (New York, 1953), p. 74.

34. The Reverend Francis Retka, "Catholic Schools in Polish Parishes," *CEA Bulletin,* 9 (Nov. 1912), 421. Retka asserts a proportion approaching one fifth, but 10 percent is more realistic.

35. Moynihan, *The Life of Archbishop John Ireland,* p. 76.

36. *Patryota* (Philadelphia), Jan. 1, 1912.

37. Ibid., Jan. 19, 1912.

38. *Słońce* (Minneapolis), June 14, 1900; and *Ameryka-Echo* (Toledo), Dec. 12, 1903.

39. *Słońce,* June 14, 1900.

40. The Reverend Z. Peszkowski, "List of Polish Roman Catholic Parishes in the United States," *Sacrum Poloniae Millenium,* 6 (Rome, 1959), 291–292.

41. Retka, "Catholic Schools," pp. 421–422.

42. Joseph Lopreato, *Italian-Americans* (New York, 1970), p. 156; and M. Mark Stolarik, "Immigration and Urbanization: The Slovak Experience, 1870–1918" (unpub. doctoral dissertation, University of Minnesota, 1974), p. 160.

43. Galush, "Forming Polonia," p. 180 shows that a majority of 78 percent (combined sample) of immigrant children had at least some parish schooling in Minneapolis, Cleveland, and Utica. There were local variations.

44. James A. Burns, *Growth and Development of the Catholic School System in the United States* (New York, 1912), pp. 324–325.

45. Joseph A. Wytrwal, *Poles in American History and Tradition* (Detroit, 1969), p. 322. Some 30,000 Polish-Americans served in the Polish Army in France.

46. *Ks. Prot. Komitetu Obywatelskiego dla Armyi Polskiej we Francji* (Utica, Polish Community Center), Oct. 16, 1917.

47. *Przewodnik Katolicki* (New Britain, Conn.), Jan. 21, 1923.

48. Ibid., Apr. 20, 1923.

49. The example of Archbishop John Krol, the first Polish-American cardinal, comes to mind. Pressure for more Polonian bishops still appears occasionally. See, for example, *Post-Eagle*, June 18, 1975.

50. E. Zdrojewski, "Szkolnictwo polskie na obczyźnie," *Kwartalnik Instytutu Naukowego do Bandań Emigracji i Kolonizacji,* 2 (Jan.-Mar. 1927), pp. 146–147.

51. E.g., *Wiadomości Cozienne* (Cleveland), Mar. 22, 1917 [on Chicago]; and *Ameryka-Echo,* Aug. 26, 1923 [on Buffalo].

52. John Higham, *Strangers in the Land: Patterns of American Nativism, 1860–1925* (New York, 1966), p. 260.

53. Zdrojewski, "Szkolnictwo," p. 147.

54. Ibid.; and Galush, "Forming Polonia," pp. 175–176.

55. Galush, "Forming Polonia," p. 182.

56. E.g., *Kuryer Polski,* June 9, 1915; and *Ameryka-Echo,* Sept. 19, 1903.

57. *Kuryer Polski,* Sept. 16, 1915. Editors also appreciated the need for a good knowledge of English. See also *Polonia w Ameryce* (Cleveland), Nov. 16, 1905.

58. Galush, "Forming Polonia," p. 180; and Andrew M. Greeley and Peter H. Rossi, *The Education of Catholic Americans* (New York, 1966), p. 37.

59. Galush, "Forming Polonia," pp. 256–261.

60. Galush, "The Polish National Catholic Church," pp. 148–149. *Album sześćdziesiątej rocznicy* (Scranton, 1957) is the basis for these calculations by decade.

61. E.g., *PNA Commericial Club Bulletin* (Minneapolis), May 1927. This was the official organ of a business/professional group of mainly second-generation Polish-Americans.

62. Galush, "Forming Polonia," p. 304.

63. Ibid., p. 305.

64. Harold J. Abramson, *Ethnic Diversity in Catholic America* (New York, 1973), pp. 52–56.

65. Harold J. Abramson, "The Religioethnic Factor and the American Experience: Another Look at the Third Generation Hypothesis," *Ethnicity,* 2 (June 1975). 168–170.

Chapter 6

# Immigration, Education, and the Social Mobility of Slovaks, 1870–1930

M. Mark Stolarik

In the last few decades the social mobility of ethnic groups in American society has drawn the attention of numerous scholars from a variety of disciplines. Their research has raised some important questions about the nature and meaning of this phenomenon. Particularly influential has been the work of the sociologists Seymour Martin Lipset and Reinhard Bendix. In their *Social Mobility in Industrial Society*,[1] Lipset and Bendix demonstrated that moving up or down the socioeconomic ladder was an integral and continuing aspect of the process of industrialization. They did not explain, however, what caused some people to move up, others to remain where they were, and others still to move down. Josef J. Barton, trained in both history and sociology, sought to answer these questions by comparing the relative rates of movement of three ethnic groups in Cleveland in his *Peasants and Strangers: Italians, Rumanians and Slovaks in an American City, 1890–1950.*[2] Barton found that education, family size, and the occupation of the father played a pivotal role in the traditional American "success story." The Romanians, who came from peasant backgrounds similar to that of the Slovaks and Italians, stressed extended public education for their children, they limited the size of their families, and their fathers tended to move from blue-collar to white-collar occupa-

103

tions more often than did Italians or Slovaks. As a result, more than 50 percent of Romanian children moved from manual to non-manual employment in the period 1900–1950 while fewer than 20 percent of Italians and Slovaks did so.[3]

What Barton did not explain was why the Romanians had such a strong commitment to education and to small families and why the fathers were so mobile in contrast to Italians and Slovaks. Part of the answer lies in the Old World background of the various immigrant groups and in their attitude toward life as molded by their religions. The Slovak experience illustrates this hypothesis.

Before the mass migration of Slovaks to America began in the 1880s, lay leaders in the Old World had stressed the value of education for social mobility, and their people seemed to agree with them. As early as 1845, for example, Ján Čipka, a student at Vienna's polytechnic institute, anticipated the abolition of serfdom and urged his countrymen to prepare themselves for the approaching industrial age by sending their children to technical schools.[4] The editors of *Národný hlásnik* (National Watchman), a monthly published in Slovakia, agreed and in subsequent decades urged the founding of Slovak trade and high schools.[5] The editors of *Obzor* (Horizon), a tri-monthly which preached self-help to Slovak peasants and craftsmen, added the sobering comment that "knowledge is power."[6]

Reacting to the urgings of their leaders, the Slovak people built and supported educational institutions whenever possible. By 1870 they had established three *gymnasia* (high schools) and operated 1,822 religious grammar schools, with the result that every second village had its own schoolhouse. So successful was the Slovak educational system that by 1885 it enrolled 88 percent of all children in its districts, the highest percentage in the entire Kingdom of Hungary.[7]

The Hungarian government, rather than applauding such efforts, attempted to thwart them because they conflicted with its official policy of Magyarization. Shortly after they reached the famous *Ausgleich* of 1867 with the Habsburgs, the Magyars of Hungary set out to assimilate their subject nationalities by attacking their school systems. In 1874 they closed the three *gymnasia* on the pretext that they propagated "Pan-Slavism." Further-

more, the Minister of Education seized upon the fact that many
village schools were poorly constructed and overcrowded in
order to nationalize them and turn them into public institutions.
By 1905 the Slovaks of Hungary had only 241 primary confes-
sional schools left under their control.[8]

Not only did the Magyars turn Slovak schools into public institutions, but they also sought to eradicate the use of all non-
Magyar languages in them. In 1877 the Hungarian parliament banned all non-Magyar texts and two years later made the teaching of
Magyar compulsory in all schools. Furthermore, starting in 1881
it paid teachers a bonus of 100 gold forints, equivalent to a year's
wages, if they did a good job in Magyarizing their pupils. Those
teachers who refused to cooperate were fired, and students who
balked at the new rules were expelled. The net result was a decline in Slovak literacy from 88 percent in 1885 to 76 percent in
1911. By the First World War, the Magyar public school system
had virtually destroyed education in the Slovak language.[9]

While the Hungarian government worked at assimilating its
subject nationalities in the late nineteenth and early twentieth
centuries, a very large section of the population began to emigrate
to America. Poor economic conditions in the Old World compelled hundreds of thousands of Slovaks to seek a livelihood in
the New. By 1920 more than 600,000 of them lived in America,
toiling in the mines, mills, and refineries of the industrial
Northeast. They were followed by a small group of intellectuals,
both lay and religious, who fled national persecution in Hungary
and who were determined to preserve Slovak life in the United
States.

Educational conditions in Hungary had a profound effect upon
the thinking of those intellectuals who left America. They brought
with them an understandable contempt for public schools, an attitude which they expressed in their publications. For example, the non-denominational *Amerikánsko-slovenské noviny*
(American-Slovak Gazette), the largest and most influential
Slovak newspaper in America before 1914, published five major
articles concerned with education between the years 1893 and
1902 which offered nine discrete statements about it. Four of the
articles declared the purpose of education to be the preservation
of the children's language and nationality, three stressed the

moral value of education, and only one affirmed schooling to be a process of self-improvement. Only once did the editors suggest that parents send their children to public schools if no parochial ones existed. The main complaint the editors made was that public schools "assimilate our children and turn them against their parents."[10]

An analysis of the *Národný kalendár* (National Almanac), an annual organ of the secular National Slovak Society, reveals similar opinions in four articles concerned with education between 1899 and 1917. Three of six ideas articulated in these articles stressed the need to preserve the children's language and heritage through schools, one emphasized the need to preserve the student's morals through schooling, while only one each pointed to the value of education for self-improvement and social mobility.[11] Indeed, one contributor denounced public schools because "whether in America or in Hungary, [they] denationalize our children."[12] Thus, secular Slovak leaders in the United States no longer shared the enthusiasm for education that their colleagues back home had expressed in earlier decades.

Religious leaders, on the other hand, underscored the moral value of education. In the Old World even the Lutheran editors of *Dom a škola* (Home and School) labeled public schools as "bastard children of the church and state." They quite correctly charged the government with using state schools to "wage war upon the nationalities," and they demanded a return to good religious instruction because "a moral upbringing is the chief aim of school and education is only a means of achieving this end."[13] Roman Catholic editors agreed that the chief aim of schooling was to instill "morality" in children. However, since most of their educational journals in Hungary were sponsored by the government, they extended this aim to include not only piety and good behavior but also loyalty to the Magyar state.[14]

Slovak Catholic leaders in America, meanwhile, cared little about loyalty to the Magyar state, but they did continue to stress the moral value of education. Between the years 1902 and 1911, for instance, *Jednota* (Union), the leading Catholic Slovak newspaper, published seventeen articles concerned with education, and these contained thirty-one statements about its worth. Eleven times the editors praised parochial schools for cultivating their children's morality, and an equal number of times they emphasized the role of such institutions in preserving the next generation's ethnicity. Only three statements admitted the value of education for social mobility, and only once did they speak of schooling as a means of self-improvement. And, while on three occasions the editors pointed to the good example set by other nationalities in parochial education, only twice did they suggest sending Slovak children to non-Slovak Catholics schools if they had none of their own.[15]

The *Kalendár Jednota* (Union Almanac), a publication of the First Catholic Slovak Union, was even more emphatic about the moral value of education. This annual published eight articles about schooling between 1898 and 1917 which contained fifteen statements about its worth. Eight of them stressed the role of Catholic institutions in cultivating a child's morality, while four added that they also preserved the children's nationality. Only once did a statement appear which praised education as a vehicle for social mobility. Similarly, only once did an author suggest that children attend public schools or parochial schools of another nationality if they had none of their own.[16] Clearly, then, Catholic leaders valued parochial schools above all else, they worried much more about their children's moral and national upbringing than about social mobility, and they had no use for public schools.

Indeed, when one looks at the reaction of Slovak Roman Catholic priests toward state schools, one finds only the harshest condemnation of these institutions. The Reverend Andrej Pavčo of Scranton, Pennsylvania, for instance, blamed the supposed decline of morality in America at the turn of the century on the "anti-religious" nature of public schools which "made loafers of all girls who attended them."[17] Father Štefan Furdek of Cleveland agreed and further charged that state schools provided "an anti-God education" with the result that America had the highest divorce rate in the world.[18] Father Ján Porubský of Binghamton, New York, claimed that "life is a preparation for God" and American public schools ignored this, causing the United States to lead the world in immorality and crime. Porubský especially singled out trade schools because they allegedly produced "illiterate" children and propagated "atheism." He concluded that "these are the places from which cities get their vagabonds, suburbs their tramps and murderers and the gallows their offerings."[19]

In a more subtle article the Reverend Štefan Furdek analyzed both school systems and, in condemning public institutions, revealed the basis of his Catholic philosophy. Public schools, he pointed out, were free. They supplied books and clothes to poor children and had nurses to care for the sick. Classes consisted of only thirty to forty pupils taught by teachers with diplomas and a good command of English. Slovak parochial schools, on the other hand, required the parents to pay tuition, their classes were overcrowded, and the teachers often lacked diplomas. In spite of these faults, Furdek found parochial schools superior to public ones because they taught catechism. He declared that "the saving of souls is more important than a good secular education." In other words, schools did not exist to promote social mobility but to give the child a decent moral upbringing. He closed his argument with the revealing statement that "a Gypsy cannot read music, but he can sure play the violin!"[20]

Since both secular and religious leaders of the Slovak community in America had such negative attitudes toward public schools and since the majority of Slovaks (80 percent) were Roman Catholics, it became almost inevitable that they would build as many parochial schools as possible and that they would send their children to these or to other Catholic institutions. The first Slovak Catholic school was built in Streator, Illinois, in 1889. By 1930, more than half of the 241 Slovak parishes in America had their own schools.[21] Furthermore, Josef Barton and I have discovered that wherever the Slovak community had its own school, as at St. Wendelin's parish in Cleveland or at St. Peter's in Fort William, now Thunder Bay, Ontario, the majority (between 60 and 80 percent) of eligible Slovak children attended it.[22] Where they did not have their own school, as at St. Cyril's in Minneapolis before 1938, almost half of the children went to parochial schools of other nationalities.[23] Thus, whenever possible, Slovak parents heeded the advice of their leaders and sent their children to parochial schools.

Slovak parents also seemed to agree with their priests' teachings that the chief aim of schooling was not necessarily to promote social mobility here on earth but to prepare for the afterlife. Thus, once a Slovak child had learned the "three R's" and knew his catechism, extended schooling became superfluous. This was clearly evident in the school attendance records of Slovak children in Cleveland, Minneapolis, and Thunder Bay. In all three cities more than 60 percent of these children dropped out between the sixth and ninth grades in the period 1910–1940. This contrasted with an average American drop-out rate of 44 percent over the same period. Only 20 percent of the Slovak children graduated from high school.[24] A few lay leaders recognized this phenomenon and complained about it. Jozef Joščák, editor of *Národné noviny* (National Gazette), accused his American countrymen of "caring less about education than had Slovaks in the Old Country."[25] Pavel Jamarik, a perceptive social critic, charged that American-Slovak parents "only sent their children to high school if they wanted them to become priests."[26] Finally, Michal Bosák, a banker and one of America's first Slovak millionaires, advised parents at least to send their youngsters to commercial schools instead of into the mines and factories so as to enable them to compete in America's capitalist society.[27] Such advice often fell on deaf ears, for, as Jozef Joščák had earlier concluded, American Slovaks "had their minds on other things."[28]

The "other things" that Joščák referred to were a way of life that rejected the basic tenets of the "Protestant ethic." In his celebrated book, *The Protestant Ethic and the Spirit of Capitalism*,[29] the German sociologist Max Weber observed that Catholic and Protestant peoples at the turn of the century had different attitudes toward life, and he developed an elaborate theory to explain these differences. Among other things, Weber theorized that the Protestant Reformation, especially its Calvinist branch, helped bring about the modern capitalist world because Calvinists regarded work as a glorification of God rather than as a curse that followed the fall of Adam, as medieval Catholics had believed. Furthermore, Weber continued, since Calvinists believed in predestination, they stressed self-discipline, education, and a constant striving to improve one's position in life. If one did improve oneself, the Calvinists believed, it was proof that one was saved because God's grace descended only upon the "elect."

Weber's theory has caused considerable debate in academic circles, with some scholars arguing that he was correct and others denouncing his views. One of his most enthusiastic defenders has been Gerhard Lenski. In his *The Religious Factor: A Sociological Study of Religion's Impact on Politics, Economics and Family Life,*[30] Lenski focused on 658 Detroit residents of various religious persuasions and sought to test the Weber thesis. He found that the Protestants in his sample constantly strove harder to succeed and to climb the socioeconomic ladder than did Catholics, and they were successful in doing so much more often than Catholics. Thus, he concluded that Weber was essentially correct. The Catholics, Lenski added, were held back by an attitude that stressed the afterlife rather than success in this world.

On the other hand, many more critics have attacked Weber's theories. Lipset and Bendix, for instance, argued that ethnicity was far more important than religious persuasion in American social mobility. They attributed the low rate of social mobility of Eastern Europeans as compared to white Anglo-Saxon Protestants to the later arrival of the former to this country. It was only a matter of time, they asserted, before third- and fourth-generation Poles, Italians, and Slovaks would catch up with British and Scandinavian peoples in the United States.[31] Similarly, the Reverend Andrew M. Greeley, in *Religion and Career: A Study of College Graduates,*[32] bent over backwards to try to disprove both Weber's and Lenski's theories. By using the resources of the National Opinion Research Center (NORC), which had administered questionnaires to 33,000 college graduates in 1961, Greeley tried to show that Catholics and Protestants had basically the same goals and aspirations in life and that one was as likely to be successful as the other. He did admit, however, that arriving Catholic immigrants may have been influenced by what he called a "folk element" which was anti-intellectual, but he saw this rapidly disappearing.[33]

There are, however, several flaws in Greeley's research. First of all, the sample he used tested only college graduates' opinions, not their actual performances. Opinions do not necessarily reflect what people do after they graduate. Nor are the opinions of college graduates a good indicator of what the rest of their ethnic community may be thinking. Furthermore, the students may have answered the questions according to what they guessed was expected of them by a society that worships social mobility. Greeley also did not differentiate enough between ethnic groups. I suspect that the vast majority of his Catholic students were German and Irish. These two peoples have been in America much longer than Eastern Europeans, they have had greater contact with white Anglo-Saxon Protestants in the past, both in the Old World and in the New, and they may even have begun to accept the "Protestant ethic" as they have gradually assimilated into American society. Finally, Greeley paid no attention to what the Catholic Church has been teaching its people about the goal of life.

Let us focus on the last point for the moment. Recall the advice of Father Porubský that "life is a preparation for God" and Father Furdek's pronouncement that "the saving of souls is much more important than a good secular education."[34] Should we dismiss these as the words of a couple of naïve priests, or do they represent official Church teaching? *The Baltimore Catechism,* which until Vatican II had been more important to most American Catholics than the Bible since it was used in most parochial schools, essentially repeats Porubský's and Furdek's teachings. In the first lesson, dealing with the purpose of life, the question is asked, "Why did God make us?" The answer given is: "God made us to show forth His goodness and to share with us His everlasting happiness in heaven." The next question asks, "What must we do to gain the happiness of heaven?" and the reply is ". . . we must know, love and serve God in this world."[35] Nowhere does it say that Catholics must strive to better themselves on this earth, to work hard, to study and make money, and to climb the social ladder. Indeed, the only mention of "work" in the *Catechism* is a derogatory one. In the lesson on the creation and fall of man, we read that because of Adam's original sin, "we have to die, to suffer to study, to work . . .!"[36] In other words, studying and work are a curse that Adam brought upon man because of his disobedience to God. This teaching is the exact opposite of the so-called Protestant ethic, and it has reached and influenced millions of Catholics over the last century.

"Success" in America has traditionally been viewed through

white Anglo-Saxon Protestant eyes. Sociologists who measure
success reflect such a bias. They always look for people moving
up from blue-collar to white-collar and thence to professional occupations. A corollary is that once one "succeeds," one moves
out of the central city to the more affluent suburbs. This pattern
of "up and out" is usually accepted as the only meaningful form
of social mobility in America.[37]

There is another approach to life, however, one seldom discussed by American scholars, which is typified by the Catholic
Slovak experience. Josef Barton discovered it in his study of Romanians, Italians, and Slovaks in Cleveland, although he did not
pursue the subject to its conclusion. Thus, in looking at the ways
in which the three immigrant groups reacted to the American
situation, Barton found that almost half of the Slovak men in his
sample became skilled workers and/or acquired some property in
their original neighborhoods of settlement. Furthermore, they
had large families which often lived in the extended form, and this
increased their overall family income.[38] Here, then, was a different way of "making it." It was all right to be a blue-collar
worker, to drop out of school at an early age, and to live in
the same neighborhood all your life. Stability, rather than movement, characterized the people of this community, and they
seemed to be satisfied with it. Even though Barton recognized
that he had discovered a different approach to social mobility, he
did not really approve of it. The Romanian example of "up and
out" impressed him as the "classic rise" of an immigrant group,
and he left the impression that somehow the Slovaks had made a
mistake.[39]

Whether or not they had made a mistake depends largely upon
their and the observer's perception of life. We might profitably in-
quire whether it is better to strive constantly to improve oneself
through education, work, and the accumulation of wealth here on
earth than to lead a moral life, to accept one's status, no matter
how low, and to strive for the higher goal of everlasting salvation.
The answer is usually very personal but much depends on the
teachings of one's church and on one's own religiosity. The majority of Slovak Catholics were very religious and did heed the
teachings of their leaders and the Church, at least in the first two
generations. Thus, they cared more for the moral upbringing of

their children than for success here on earth, and this was reflected in their condemnation of public schools, in their praise for Catholic education, and in their acceptance of blue-collar work and life in ethnic neighborhoods.

But what of third- and fourth-generation American Slovaks? Do they perceive life in the same way as their parents and grandparents? Do they have the same attitudes toward work and school, family, and neighborhood? We do not know because no one has yet researched this group. If Andrew Greeley's studies of Germans and Irish Catholics are correct, then perhaps the "Protestant ethic" will eventually rub off on Slovak Catholics as they become more assimilated into American society. Perhaps the growing nationwide decline in parochial school attendance will aid this process. Indeed, Catholic values generally may be changing across the land, and the third and fourth generations may reflect such changes. These are questions which await further research.

Should someone still be skeptical about the whole theory of the "Protestant ethic," he might study the various components of the Slovak community in America. According to the best estimates available, three-quarters of the Slovak population in America in 1930 was Roman Catholic, almost 15 percent was Lutheran, and the rest was divided between Greek Catholics and Reformed. The attitudes of Slovak Lutherans and Calvinists toward life, work, education, and their social mobility could be compared and contrasted with that of their Catholic counterparts. Such a study would supercede previous efforts because one would not have to control for ethnicity, time of arrival, and other variables except religion. Such research could, hopefully, deal with the whole theory of the "Protestant ethic" to everyone's satisfaction.

Finally, the American concept of social mobility needs closer scrutiny. Should the majority of scholars continue to accept without question the ideal that everyone should constantly strive to move "up and out"? What are the social consequences of such a philosophy? Is it good and necessary that everyone seek a higher education, for example? Who will sweep the streets, collect the garbage, fix the roads, and man the factories if we continue to revere non-manual work so much? And, what are the consequences of an upwardly mobile white-collar worker moving from neighborhood to neighborhood and city to city all the time in order to keep climbing? Is this good for his family? Does it not in fact destroy extended family solidarity and breed an intense nuclear family that has no roots and no sense of community?[40] Indeed, the historian Rowland Berthoff has argued that America has in the past suffered from too much mobility, and he predicted that this country's many social ills would not disappear until a sense of community was restored in this land. This implied that Americans would have to stop moving around so much.[41] In this respect those Eastern Europeans who have stayed put and have tried to preserve their neighborhoods have been in the vanguard of social planning. Perhaps Michael Novak is right. Perhaps we should stress extended family life, ethnic neighborhoods, stability, and quietness again.[42] At least we should let those who prefer this way of life live in peace, without bureaucratic harassment. This would mean fighting "block-busting," "red-lining," freeway construction, and any other threats to community life that individuals or the government may pose. In short, it would call for respect for the pluralism of American life. It would mean toleration for the Catholic alternative to the "Protestant ethic."

## Notes

1. Seymour Martin Lipset and Reinhard Bendix, *Social Mobility in Industrial Society,* (Berkeley, 1959).

2. Josef J. Barton, *Peasants and Strangers: Italians, Rumanians and Slovaks in an American City, 1890–1950* (Cambridge, Mass., 1975).

3. Ibid., pp. 99–100.

4. *Slovenskje národňje novini* (Bratislava), Nov. 18, 1845, p. 125.

5. *Národný hlásnik* (Martin), Aug. 31, 1868, p. 178; Oct. 31, 1868, p. 225; and May 31, 1871, p. 135.

6. *Obzor* (Skalica), Jan. 5, 1872, and Jan. 5, 1881.

7. Július Mésároš et al., *Dejiny Slovenska II: Od roku 1848 do 1900* (Bratislava, 1968), p. 264, and *Dom a škola* (Ružomberok), 3 (1887), 23–25.

8. *Zipser Botte* (Levoča), No. 29, 1905, and Jozef Gregor-Tajovský, "Východné Slovensko," *Národný kalendár, 1913* (Pittsburgh), pp. 243–244.

9. Minister of Education to the School Inspector of Spiš, Slovak State Archives in Levoča, County Spiš, Executive Council, 420, KB, 1877; ibid., 462, 1881; ibid., II, 181, 1898; ibid., II, 183, 1902. See also U.S.

Congress, Senate, *Reports of the Immigration Commission*, 3, 61st Cong., 3d sess., 1911, Senate Document 756, p. 84, for literacy rates.

10. *Amerikánsko-slovenské noviny* (Pittsburgh), Feb. 2, 1893, p. 6; Dec. 8, 1894, p. 8; Jan. 8, 1895, p. 1; July 13, 1895, p. 4; and Apr. 28, 1898, p. 8. The quotation is from the first article.

11. *Národný kalendár, 1899*, pp. 44–45; *1911*, pp. 59–64 and 224–228; *1917*, pp. 222–224.

12. Ibid., *1917*, p. 222.

13. *Dom a škola*, 2 (1886), 194; and 3 (1887), 73.

14. See for example *Naša zástava* (Prešov) Sept. 20, 1908, p. 2; Oct. 4, 1908, p. 2; *Eperjes* (Prešov), Sept. 1, 1913, p. 1; Aug. 15, 1913, p. 2; Oct. 15, 1914, p. 3; *Egyház és iskola* (Prešov), Feb. 15, 1918, p. 69.

15. *Jednota* (Cleveland), Sept. 17, 1902, p. 3; Oct. 1, 1902, p. 4; Aug. 31, 1904, p. 4; July 12, 1905, p. 4; July 26, 1905, p. 4; Aug. 9, 1905, p. 4; Feb. 7, 1906, p. 4; July 1, 1908, p. 4; Aug. 19, 1908, p. 4; Sept. 8, 1909, p. 4; Feb. 16, 1910, p. 4; Mar. 23, 1910, p. 4; July 27, 1910, p. 4; Aug. 17, 1910, p. 4; Sept. 2, 1910, p. 4; Apr. 5, 1911, p. 4; and Aug. 23, 1911, p. 4.

16. *Kalendár Jednota, 1898* (Cleveland), pp. 133–134; *1899*, pp. 135–136; *1902*, pp. 128–136; *1907*, pp. 120–123; *1908*, pp. 177–178; *1911*, pp. 29–31; *1913*, pp. 123–128; and *1917*, pp. 83–85.

17. Ibid., *1898*, p. 133.

18. *Jednota*, July 12, 1905, p. 4.

19. *Kalendár Jednota, 1907*, pp. 120–123.

20. *Jednota*, Aug. 19, 1908, p. 4.

21. *Národnie noviny* (Martin), Oct. 5, 1889, p. 3, and Oct. 23, 1890, p. 3; *Kalendár Jednota, 1930*, pp. 193–201.

22. Barton, *Peasants and Strangers*, pp. 149–150; M. Mark Stolarik, "Immigration and Urbanization: The Slovak Experience, 1870–1918" (unpub. doctoral dissertation, University of Minnesota, 1974), pp. 165–166.

23. Stolarik, "Immigration and Urbanization," pp. 165–166.

24. Barton, *Peasants and Strangers*, pp. 132 and 137, and Stolarik, "Immigration and Urbanization," p. 170.

25. *Národné noviny* (Pittsburgh), June 2, 1910, p. 4.

26. Pavel Jamarik, *Výchova dietok. Praktické návody pre slovenských rodičov* (author's publication, Disputant, Virginia, 1913), p. 22.

27. *Kalendár Jednota, 1917*, pp. 83–85.

28. *Národné noviny*, June 2, 1910, p. 4.

29. Trans. by Talcott Parsons (London, 1930).

30. Gerhard Lenski, *The Religious Factor: A Sociological Study of Religion's Impact on Politics, Economics and Family Life* (New York, 1961).

31. *Social Mobility in Industrial Society*, pp. 49–52.

32. Andrew M. Greeley, *Religion and Career: A Study of College Graduates* (New York, 1963).

33. Ibid., p. 134.

34. See note 19, sup.

35. The Reverend Michael A. McGuire, *The New Baltimore Catechism and Mass* (No. 2, Official Revised Edition, New York, 1941), p. 14.

36. Ibid., p. 29.

37. All the scholars cited above—Lipset and Bendix, Lenski, Greeley, and even Barton—accept this pattern. One who questions its wisdom is Richard Sennett in *Families Against the City: Middle Class Homes in Industrial Chicago, 1872–1890* (Cambridge, Mass., 1970).

38. Barton, *Peasants and Strangers*, p. 143.

39. Ibid., pp. 172–173.

40. This was part of Richard Sennett's argument in *Families Against the City*.

41. See Rowland Berthoff, *An Unsettled People: Social Order and Disorder in American History* (New York, 1971).

42. Michael Novak makes this argument in *The Rise of the Unmeltable Ethnics: Politics and Culture in the Seventies* (New York, 1971) and again in two Ethnic Millions Political Action Committee (EMPAC!) statements of 1973 and 1975.

Chapter 7

# Western Impact on East European Jews
## A Philadelphia Fragment

Maxwell Whiteman

Conditions in the clothing trade in the last two decades of the nineteenth century were notorious in American labor history. The unwholesome sweatshop system and its many destructive effects are associated with the rise of the Jewish labor movement in New York. Philadelphia differed only in the lesser number of people involved, and in the early participation of the rabbinate in the struggles that brought an organized trade union movement to the clothing and allied trades. The conditions of a long working day, low pay, squalor, disease, and home contracting were identical.[1]

If the immigrant clothing workers of Philadelphia were spared the evils of New York tenement life, they found little to boast of in terms of better living or working conditions. Technological developments that speeded the manufacture of ready-made clothing did not improve their lives. At each level of work, contractors, subcontractors, and their hands were wedged helplessly into a highly competitive seasonal market. Contractors sweated their profits from the earnings of the immigrant mass. When finished garments were returned to the manufacturer, one contractor was pitted ruthlessly against another by the manufacturer for a further cut in production costs. Squeezed to reduce their pay by the contractors, the immigrant workers submitted to a longer work

117

day to compensate for the loss. Fifty percent of Philadelphia's ready-made clothing was produced by this grinding process which started the day a piece of cloth was cut and ended the day a completed garment was pressed and returned to the manufacturer.

The Jews who had been driven from Russia to the United States in the early 1880s were introduced to circumstances which they could not have envisioned when they fled their old homes. They had exchanged oppression for a new misery: the trauma of adjusting to the occupations of a new land and facing manufacturers who gorged themselves on the profits of a continuous supply of cheap and seemingly content labor.

The Jewish immigrants thought of life as a cycle that began with blessing the incoming Sabbath and ended with the *havdalah* service welcoming the new week. For those employed in the clothing trade, even these ceremonies were marred by the need to work on the Sabbath. The mercilessly long week that followed was brightened only by the lingering memory of Sabbath candles which not only illuminated their dingy homes, but glowed on their narrow world.

Most immigrants of the early eighties had had no exposure to secular education. They were trained in Bible but were not biblical scholars. Their mother tongue was Yiddish, but they knew little of the renascence of Yiddish literature. Only a few grasped the social or economic implications of labor unions, for which they had but little time to spare. They looked upon strikes, which had become prevalent in heavy industry and in transportation, as an interference with one's livelihood—at best as inexplicable foolishness.[2]

Before the eighties had come to an end, however, the immigrants began to show their restiveness. They had come to comprehend the value of a dollar and were no longer intrigued by comparing a kopek with a penny, they discovered food other than potatoes and herring, witnessed the incoming of thousands of their countrymen, and probed the complex urban world surrounding them. Though only a small number were able to abandon the sweatshop or flee the clothing trade for other means of earning a living, their eagerness to plant roots in the New World was immeasurable. Unobtrusively and independently, they organized one society after another to express their inner yearnings. Their determination to overcome their economic plight, to compensate for the hard work week, and to find a niche of comfort in their immediate circle led to the establishment of religious and secular organizations that characterized Jewish immigrant life in the southern section of the city.

Within this self-created network of social, cultural, and religious institutions, clothing workers, cigarmakers, bakers, and peddlers met to discuss all manner of problems. So long as the immigrant activity was confined to religious and social institutions, the numerous *landsmanshaftn* and mutual aid societies were looked upon by all with patronizing satisfaction. Trade unions and political clubs, wrote one contemporary, "are discountenanced by the Jewish community," meaning of course the established Jews who had come from Germany. When Russian Jews sought to unionize, when their discontent was no longer muffled, their efforts were condemned by the older Jewish residents and rejected by the Gentile-dominated clothing trade unions.[3]

Not only did the immigrants dress differently and speak a language described as a raucous jargon by those unfamiliar with it, their religious practices bewildered many of the descendants of older Jewish residents. The religious differences were obvious even to the casual observer. Members of the prestigious Spanish-Portuguese Congregation Mikveh Israel, who reached the highest social position of any group of Jews in Philadelphia at that time, clung to an ancient form of worship uncommon to Jews from Western Europe, whose different interpretation of observances and attachment to a German milieu produced congregations where a Jewish sermon still was delivered in German. This was in sharp contrast with the English sermon spoken at Mikveh Israel.[4]

Among the Russians worship was personal, uninhibited, and free of the meticulous restraint at Mikveh Israel or in the synagogues of Western Jewry. In their initial contacts on American soil Jews of different European background appeared as strangers among themselves. Although Jews were not regarded as separatists in religion, they were sharply divided in their practices. The orthodox synagogues of the East Europeans, ramshackle establishments sitting in the midst of poverty, reflected the variations of their former homes. Though their members shared a common liturgy, their pronunciation of Hebrew and their intonation of prayers varied considerably and revealed the localities from which they came. It was as much a subject for wonder to other Jews that the immigrant body would band together on the basis of liturgy and rites, localisms and geography, as it was a source of comfort to the newcomers to join together on the basis of familiar customs. And what governed the mushrooming of synagogues also influenced the rise of mutual aid societies. Held together by the bonds of secularized philanthropy, organizations like the United Hebrew Charities looked at the immigrants more as clients than as fellow Jews. Economic, social, and religious divisions imperiled cooperation between them.[5]

The most serious intrusion in the lives of immigrant workers was their inability to offset the erosive influence of their occupations on traditional religious habits. They had no established leadership to guide them, and none of the central authority to which they had been accustomed. Whatever rabbinical authority existed could not counter the economic and industrial forces that engulfed the daily lives of the immigrants. They were slowly deprived of the right of Sabbath observance, denied the time for their daily prayers, and thrust into the world of other experiences.

The history of the East European rabbinate at this time is brief. Israel Sachs, a forceful speaker and a respected Talmudist who might have provided the necessary leadership, died prematurely in 1889. The considerable influence claimed for him during his four years in Philadelphia came as the result of his combat against the denigrating effects of the new society on his fellow immigrants. His concern was for the gravity of breaking the Sabbath, the speed with which males discarded their religious garments, and the lack of a religious school system. However, he never challenged the economic roots that brought about these problems. Indeed, Sachs is not known to have shown an interest in the worsening conditions of the clothing trade.[6]

Members of the rabbinate who were motivated by the awesome social forces at the end of the century were molded by different backgrounds and other experiences. The Reform rabbinate in 1885 articulated its principles on social justice and focused upon the redemption of man from "hunger and wretchedness." Joseph Krauskopf of Keneseth Israel was its foremost exponent in Philadelphia. These views evolved from prophetic teaching but they became so commingled with the teachings of the social gospel of American Protestants that their aims were diluted by glowing phrases emphasizing common creedal beliefs. The flow of sermonic oratory never reached down to the Eastern European Jewish immigrant, and whatever influence social justice and social gospel had upon the general public, it never touched the sweatshop.[7]

Religious traditionalism, commonly referred to as orthodoxy, was represented by Sabato Morais, the Italian-born minister of Mikveh Israel. He too looked to the teachings of the Prophets for inspiration, but his views, which approached more closely a pattern of social justice, never adopted that name. From the pulpit of Mikveh Israel his antebellum sermons on the plight of impoverished Jewish immigrants from Germany were followed by his attacks on slavery. He drafted a program for the relief of the first and was a consistent opponent of the second. After the Civil War he persisted in his declamations against what he believed to be unjust legislation against immigrants, such as the Oriental Exclusion Act and the mistreatment of the Chinese. To the conditions of the new Jewish immigrants, he reacted with equal fervor, condemning the opponents of immigration.[8]

One cannot surmise what the immigrants thought. Their views were shared privately with a *landsman* over a glass of tea. Their reaction to the Reform movement in Judaism was still a mystery, and though they had more affinity to the traditional observances at Mikveh Israel, its Spanish-Portuguese ritual failed to attract them. It was still too soon for the immigrant to identify the elitism of both congregations. Most difficult of all was the immigrants' lack of a public voice. Prior to 1892 there was no Philadelphia Yiddish press that could have given some indication of their simmering discontent. The newly founded *Jewish Exponent* was struggling to orient itself to the phenomenon of the Russian immigrant and straddle the conflict between Reform and traditional Judaism.[9] Trade unionism was not one of the *Jewish Exponent*'s themes. News of the attempts to organize workers in the New York apparel trades reached Philadelphia by way of the Yiddish press and the socialists of that city.[10] If they made an impression on the Philadelphians, there is scant evidence of it. During 1888, however, there is evidence of a new radicalism filtering into the Jewish quarter and agitating the clothing workers.

Older labor organizations in Philadelphia, the city where Karl Marx's First International expired with only a whimper, did not view immigrant Jewish membership favorably at this time. The older Journeymen Tailors' Union and the more recently organized Tailors' National Progressive Union did not recruit Jewish immigrants into their guild-like organizations. It is doubtful, however, if the East European Jews of the late eighties even knew of Philadelphia's labor history, or cared.

Two months after the organization of the United Hebrew Trades in New York City in October 1888, the first local bid, prompted by local conditions and personalities, was made to organize a branch of the Philadelphia Jewish clothing workers into a union of their own.[11] This movement remained independent of New York and of older Philadelphia unions. Circumstances in New York and Philadelphia were strikingly different anyway. New York's Jews had prior union experience, a lively socialist community interested in trade unions, and a Yiddish press, no matter how immature, that reported on their activity. Philadelphians lacked experience, had no voice, nor any outside support. In New York, the United Hebrew Trades, involving several unions, was organized as a result of the work of the Socialist Labor Party. In Philadelphia the socialist movement was notably weak and ineffective among Jews.

In the absence of traditional or socialist organizing, a handful of zealous anarchists shrewdly seized the initiative and propagandized the sweatshop workers in the clothing and cigar trades. Early in December 1888, at 203 Pine Street, a central meeting place for Jews, about one hundred persons responded to a call that led to the organization of the Jewish Tailors and Operators Association.[12] To the inflammatory orators imbued with the ideals of philosophical anarchism, the clothing operators were easy prey. Three youthful Philadelphia anarchists in the cigar trade, Ben Pokrass, Isidor Prenner, and Max Staller, torn from their Russian-Jewish moorings, were drawn into the vortex of American anarchism. They were convinced that Jewish workers would solve their problems by adopting anarchist principles. Building their program on demands for justice, the anarchists made deep inroads among the immigrant cigarmakers.[13]

Yet many resisted their arguments, disagreeing with their condemnation of American society and their renunciation of religion. The rabbinic scholar Moses Bayuk, whose sons founded a major cigar factory, for example, disavowed the anarchists and the cigar trade and moved to the Jewish agricultural colony of South Jersey, where he became a leader in the synagogue, pursued his studies, and contributed to the Anglo-Jewish press.[14] Samuel Paley, who worked at the same trade, licking the wrappers onto hand-rolled cigars, went on to establish a major factory of his own, later becoming associated with a major American communications industry.[15] These men were impervious to the agitation of their fiery colleagues, though they were quick to recognize personal solutions to the complexity of immigrant life.

If the anarchists' intentions were not clear to the cloakmakers, they were understood by George Randorf, the representative of the Association for the Protection of Jewish Immigrants. Randorf encouraged the organization of a protective society governed by union principles, but strongly cautioned the workers against the wave of radical ideologies that were spreading among them and undermining traditional Jewish life.[16]

The harassed members of the tailoring trade were also pressured by their employers. When their discontent became known in the shops, Gabriel Blum, president of Blum Brothers, cloakmakers, arranged a banquet at which he could counsel his employees to act moderately. He addressed his Yiddish-speaking audience in German, and urged them to form a society governed by Jewish religious principles whose object would be to provide for one another during the off-season when there was less work. Blum's advice was naïvely interpreted as support for the new union.

An informal meeting was held by the tailors, and they decided to ask the senior member of Blum Brothers to raise their wages. Their demand was based on the needs of their underfed families. Such demands, responded Gabriel Blum, were unprecedented. Outraged, he rejected the plea, admonished the committee who visited him, and warned them as fellow Jews that "the Lord God

will punish you for such conduct." One worker protested, for he
failed to see how the Heavenly One would punish men who asked
for better conditions for their children. The workers, without any
other preparation, promptly struck.[17]

The first strike of the first Jewish garment workers union lasted
two days. On the third day, the frightened, ill-used men returned
to work. Blum then demanded of them that each take an oath on
the Bible vowing never to strike again. All but one took the oath.
The tailors had lost the first round. The bungling anarchists tem-
porarily retreated, but conditions in the trade grew worse. There
was a brief respite, and then all sides girded themselves in
preparation for the first general strike of Philadelphia cloakmakers.

In their first bid to remedy their grievances, the Jewish garment
workers not only failed to improve their conditions, but were
humiliated into submission by one of the manufacturers. This was
grist for the mill of the anarchists. It enabled them to attack the
use of religion by the wealthier Jews to subvert the labor movement, and provided them with choice propaganda with which to
discredit the older Jewish families, especially those from Germany. A latent feeling of distrust characteristic of newcomers in a
strange environment had been growing before the aborted strike
of 1889. The anarchists, preying on the problems of the immigrants and eager to recoup their waning influence, attempted to
turn the distrust into open antagonism. They charged the capitalist *yahudim,* the German-Jewish bosses, with the responsibility
of bringing on many of the ills among the immigrants. Had not the
clothiers used religion as a trick to prevent a further strike? Were
they not the patrons and directors of the United Hebrew Charities
which had brought the workers to the sweatshops? Were they not
arrayed on the side of capitalism? And did they not own the
dingy, rat-infested hovels in which the immigrants lived?[18]

Such were the challenging questions of the anarchists who
were determined to keep the workers on their side, and to add
another obstacle to the social and cultural barriers that separated
the immigrants from the older Jewish residents. But in fact, these
accusations applied only to a small number of the clothiers.
Furthermore, the garment workers had little interest in a social
analysis of their conditions; they were more concerned with over-
coming the plight in which they found themselves.

The Jewish workers in the needle trades were hardly promising material for anarchist propaganda. They knew nothing of its philosophy, and even less about trade unions. They were more concerned about keeping the Sabbath, even at the risk of losing their jobs, than with the allegations against capitalist tyranny. They were sensitive to their poor and unwholesome surroundings, but to the average immigrant worker fresh from tsarist Russia, the United States was a haven.[19]

Moreover, the Jewish anarchists were strange people to the masses of immigrants. Their ideology was beyond comprehension, they exchanged Jewish dietary habits for vegetarianism or ate ritually forbidden foods, and they condemned orthodox religious practice so dear to the East Europeans. At the same time they considered their ideas and their goals the epitome of idealism.

Most of the anarchists were intellectuals rather than workers, but of necessity, they entered the cigarmaking and garment trades. In Philadelphia, where they were more influential than any other branch of the radical movement, they were divided into three groups: those who were of old American stock; the foreign-born English, Scots, and Germans; and the Jews, who were numerically the smallest.

During the early months of 1890, the anarchists carried on such a lively program among the garment workers that the Socialist Labor Party, anxious to make its own inroads, sent representatives from New York to spread propaganda among the Philadelphians. But the Socialists were weak compared to the fiery anarchist orators, who knew the workers personally.[20]

To the underpaid sweatshop workers, struggling desperately to support their families, both anarchists and Socialists offered leadership, and if they rejected the political philosophy of both, they accepted the trade union program, especially that of the anarchists. The anarchists successfully planted their seed in fertile soil. The old union was rehabilitated, and it adopted the name of Cloakmakers Union No. 1. It collected a strike fund, prepared a series of demands, and on May 16, 1890, when the clothing season was in full operation, called for a strike.[21]

Alerted by the growing unrest among the garment workers in Philadelphia, and by the sharp competition of the New York clothiers, the manufacturers had prepared themselves for any exigencies resulting from union organization by forming an organization of their own. The organization, the Philadelphia Cloak Manufacturers' Association, represented thirty-five firms. Three of the outstanding firms—Blum Brothers, Patterson, and Franklin Company—were spokesmen for the Association. Arrayed against the manufacturers were an estimated 800 immigrant Jewish strikers, none of whose length of residence in Philadelphia exceeded eight years.

Enthusiasm, courage, and an air of confidence characterized the attitude of the workers in the first days of the strike. As the days turned into weeks, however, the resources of the strikers were exhausted, and when there was no indication of a settlement, their courage waned. Some of the hard-pressed strikers turned to peddling, while others left the city to find employment elsewhere. The manufacturers, concerned with the production of the garments, were not idle and sought non-union help among immigrants, taking them from ship to shop.

There could be no doubt about the Jewish complexion of the strike when the Reverend Sabato Morais of Congregation Mikveh Israel, the most prominent Jewish minister in Philadelphia, emerged on the scene as a self-appointed arbitrator. One of Morais' first steps was to invite Rabbi Joseph Krauskopf, of Reform Congregation Keneseth Israel, and Dr. Marcus Jastrow, of Rodeph Shalom, to join in the negotiations. Their presence was vital, for a number of the manufacturers were members of the congregations over which the rabbis presided. In addition to the clergymen, George Randorf acted as Morais' aide.[22]

Randorf, an immigrant from Odessa, although he had lived in Philadelphia only two years and had not yet reached the age of thirty, earned the respect of the older community. He was an agent of the Association for the Protection of Jewish Immigrants, the Philadelphia representative of the Baron de Hirsch Fund, and the interpreter for the United States Commissioner of Immigration at the Port of Philadelphia. His rapport with the immigrants was excellent, as was his linguistic ability, which included a knowledge of Yiddish and Slavic languages. Randorf's credentials made him a choice aide for Morais.[23]

The Jewish communal structure never sanctioned the union or the strike. Curiously, the United Hebrew Charities, which worked directly with the immigrants in obtaining employment for them, securing adequate shelter for them, and providing education for their children, officially remained silent. In an age when secular matters involving Jews were of primary concern to the Jewish press, to the synagogue, and to the official bodies that represented Jewry, the silence of the United Hebrew Charities was all the more apparent. This may have been due to the fact that many of the leaders of the society were themselves clothiers, and preferred that the charities did not take sides in the issue. But the representative of the United Hebrew Charities, George Randorf, was unofficially committed to the side of the strikers, and the Charities made no attempt to restrain his activity.

The summer of 1890 was unusually hot. Tempers mounted on all sides. The situation became grave, for it was no longer a secret that the strikers who refused to compromise were starving and endangering the lives of their families. The manufacturers also were prepared to yield nothing. Newspapers found the strike sensational, and the Jews of Philadelphia, who saw it only as the washing of dirty linen in public, were deeply disturbed. At this point Morais, who commanded the respect of both sides, threw his energies into obtaining an agreement in the dispute.

In mid-July Morais mounted the pulpit of Mikveh Israel to deliver a discourse on the working conditions of the immigrants which set the tone for his feelings and which elevated the spirit of Judaism through his personal interest in the workers. No other Jewish clergyman is known to have delivered a sermon on the strike. In the midst of negotiations, Joseph Krauskopf, of Keneseth Israel, left for a vacation in Cape May, and his popular Sunday sermons were discontinued for the summer. Jastrow, who had the interest and the will to preach, was in the throes of witnessing his congregation veer in the direction of Reform Judaism and lacked the spirit to involve himself in the strike.[24] The death of Rabbi Sachs denied the immigrants the possible support or leadership which he might have offered.

Morais had long since established full freedom of the pulpit at Mikveh Israel, but now, once again, he was compelled to answer for himself in addition to speaking on behalf of the strikers and their suffering families. To those who cautioned him to refrain from action and contain his views, he replied: "May the day never dawn, when the disciples of prophets and sages, to whose keeping practical religion has been entrusted, shall be muzzled, that they may not denounce social iniquities." He chastised the wealthy manufacturers whom he had visited to discuss a settlement, the "rich individuals who still begrudged the scanty loaf ate by men and women and children herded together in rooms" unfit to live in. He told of his meeting with the manufacturers and their cold indifference as he "pleaded for my hapless brethren . . . Who will wonder that periodical strikes will break out."

He accused the manufacturers of being responsible for the slow death of the immigrants, and in general condemned their attitudes. It was a bold, searing sermon, reminiscent of those which he had delivered in support of the antislavery movement against Southern sympathizers during the Civil War, and against the injustices to which Jews had been subjected in countries with less favorable political climates. He attacked the sweating system and committed himself to the cause of the strikers.[25]

On July 19, 1890, Sabato Morais and Dr. Jastrow—Rabbi Krauskopf had not yet returned from Cape May—arranged for a meeting between the strikers and the clothing manufacturers. After many hours of negotiations the employees agreed to five of the six points demanded by the union: That the manufacturers association "acknowledge the existence of Cloakmakers Union No. I; that the union provide the manufacturers with employees, and the respective firms hire outsiders only when the union cannot fulfill its obligation; that the strikers be allowed to return to work without being discriminated against; that the rate of pay for garments be fixed in consultation with employees and that prices for piece work be posted publicly in the shops, and that the cloakmakers should not be compelled to work at night." On the sixth point, which argued that those employed during the strike should either join the union or be discharged, there was no agreement.[26]

The rabbis, anxious to resolve this final point, proposed to the manufacturers that they be permitted to address the immigrant workers who had been brought in to "scab," and explain to them the position of the union. But they were not permitted to do so. Rebuffed, Morais proceeded on his own, and in an unusual gesture, called on the non-union men in their homes and successfully induced five of them to join the union.

That evening the strikers met at their Pine Street headquarters to listen to the reports of Morais in English, Jastrow in German, and Randorf in Yiddish. Yiddish was the language they understood best. The clergymen recommended that the five points be accepted and that the men return to work immediately. They urged that the sixth point, which was tantamount to union recognition and a closed shop, be set aside for future action. The non-union men could be convinced to join the ranks of the cloakmakers after the strike was settled. Had not Morais set the example of enlisting five of the men into the union over the opposition of the manufacturers and to the embarrassment of the anarchists? But all of his arguments, including the fact that the "scabs" were newly arrived, uninformed immigrants who were also being ill-used, were of no avail. The anarchists overwhelmed him. They threw Morais' arguments back at the strikers. Isidor Prenner, the union manager and a leading anarchist, cried "no concession" as long as the "scabs" remained, and Morais' powerful plea was rejected by a unanimous no.

The meeting of 450 strikers went wild, and hours passed before the men could be calmed sufficiently to permit Morais and his associates to resume negotiations with the strikers. The manufacturers had yielded as much as Morais had been able to persuade them to, and by comparison to similar strikes in the 1880s their conduct may be described as liberal.[27] Victory was in the hands of the strikers, but their inexperience in measuring the gains of collective bargaining prevented them from recognizing success. Goaded by the anarchists into believing that victory had to be total, the strikers made one more attempt to oust the "scabs" by agreement. Bypassing Morais, an independent committee of strikers met with the manufacturers and reached a compromise whereby the "scabs" were to leave the inside shops and be given outside work, a proposal which the union was prepared to accept.

Before the strikers could grasp the meaning of their sudden success, however, it suddenly slipped through their hands. As far as the episode can be reconstructed, on Monday, August 4, a group of strikers, perhaps unaware of the agreement that had just been reached, made an attempt to prevent the "scabs" from working. The manufacturers responded by having many of the men arrested for "disturbing the peace and interfering with and threatening to do violence to the cloakmakers at work." Simultaneously, the manufacturers issued a strong manifesto against the strikers. Hopes for a peaceful settlement were shattered.

The strikers were in a precarious position. All their resources were exhausted. Their families were starving. With the exception of Morais, who still persisted in the cause of the strikers, other religious leaders did nothing or very little to relieve the suffering because they were not in sympathy with the cloakmakers. The strikers endured only because Morais collected a fund for their families, and because the butchers and bakers and grocerymen who were their relatives could not turn them away.

During the first week of August, Morais toured the southern quarter between Second and Fifth Streets, and Bainbridge and Catherine Streets. His brief report of the abject poverty, published in the *Jewish Exponent,* is a classic description of incredibly poor housing, starvation, and misery. Discontent was now widespread among the victims of the strike.[28]

The union called for a mass meeting at Wheatley Hall, at Fifth and Gaskill Streets, to protest the arrests of August 4. Prenner was the main speaker. The anarchist Max Staller chaired the meeting. The Jewish core of South Philadelphia was jammed with excited Jews who represented all points of view, and whose interest and curiosity drew them to Wheatley Hall. What no one suspected at the time was the intention of the police who surrounded the neighborhood, awaiting a signal from a turncoat striker ready to identify the anarchist leaders. At the given moment, the police burst through the doors and seized Prenner and Staller, clubbing anyone who stood in their path. Many of the members of the audience were treated severely.

Bystanders in the street fared no better. Anyone who happened to be near the police was beaten indiscriminately, arrested, and charged with the crime of anarchism. The *Public Ledger* gave a full, approving report of the police action. The *Sunday Mercury,* whose proprietor, Louis Edward Levy, was also the president of the Immigrant Association, lamented the excesses. The papers urged Jews who were not interested in the strike to proclaim their innocence and assert their patriotism. The cry of bomb-throwing anarchists which came from the clothiers was effective, and the first step in breaking the strike with the aid of the police was successful.[29]

On August 21, two weeks later, Blum Brothers and S. Simon and Company introduced a new element into the strike by employing Negroes to do outside work. The manufacturers were determined to have their fall capes and cloaks on time, as they normally did, and they accepted an "offer" from the Reverend [Richard?] Christian, a Negro clergyman, to produce the garments. In a few days, twenty-five Negro women were put to work in the minister's home. In a week the number of women was increased to eighty, and plans were made to employ no less than three hundred. It was also expected that when work was begun on plush goods their wages would average from fourteen to sixteen dollars weekly—a wage that the most industrious sweatshop contractor had never earned, and which was a bonanza for the Negroes. In a few days a large three-story building at the northwest corner of Twelfth and Locust Streets was opened as a factory, and nearly two-hundred Negro women were given employment by a number of firms.[30]

At North Wales, outside the city, the Philadelphia Suit Company hired a hall and employed fifty people to make cloaks, and the firm also announced that it would build a factory there.[31] These strike-breaking methods proved effective. S. Simon and Company was the first to announce that many of their old hands had offered to return. To counter such a return, the anarchists urged the strikers to seek work in New York City rather than yield to the manufacturers. In fact, the strikers were already doing so without the encouragement of the anarchists. Several hundred cloakmakers gathered at the offices of the United Hebrew Charities to appeal for railroad fare to New York City, but the appeal was rejected on the basis that the Charities would have to support the strikers' families. Finally, the Charities felt compelled to disperse the strikers with the aid of police. In spite of this, the strikers found their way to New York. Meanwhile, the number of striking cloakmakers remaining in the city dwindled to less than one hundred.[32]

Meetings with the manufacturers accomplished nothing. Manufacturers discouraged further meetings with the strikers. Morais, pained by the impasse and by the demoralized strikers and their starving families, now addressed the workers in writing. He repeated his former arguments, stressing the gains that might still be obtained, and pleaded with them to carry on their full union program after returning to work. His lengthy and touching letter appeared in the *Ledger and Transcript* and closed with this appeal: "Some may have gone from among you to other cities, but even if those who have left here were fully assured of a comfortable living, the majority who cannot transfer numerous children or women in ill health elsewhere, remain yet behind in a lamentable state. . . . Deliver them from starvation and ill health by a return to work which will gain for you a livelihood, and win the approval of all right thinking among the community in Philadelphia."[33]

The completely disillusioned men, whose strength was sapped after many weary months of fruitless effort, found Morais' letter easy to welcome. A few days after it was received, on Saturday morning, August 23, while Morais was reading the service at Mikveh Israel, the union sent for George Randorf, asking him to become their messenger to the manufacturers.

Randorf hurried to the synagogue on Seventh Street near Arch, and informed Morais that the strikers were prepared to negotiate a settlement whereby they could return to work at once. In deference to Morais, Randorf requested that the strikers wait until the close of the Sabbath when they would assemble at 616 Spruce Street. About fifty men, the remnant of the original eight hundred, gathered to discuss mediation with Randorf and Morais. There is no record of the anarchists' participating in this meeting. The two mediators pointed to the possibility that the manufacturers might not consent to any of the terms agreed upon earlier. Spiritless and disheartened, the strikers sought a settlement whereby they would not have to go back to work singly, but would return in a body.[34]

Morais and Randorf then called upon Sampson Simon of S. Simon and Company on Sunday morning and reached an agreement with them. On Monday, they met with Blum Brothers and the Philadelphia Suit Company and salvaged some of the points contained in the original demands. Before the day was over, the terms of the agreement had been ratified. There was to be no discrimination against the strikers; wages for piece work were to be fixed by the manufacturers at a rate higher than before; and suits now pending in court against the anarchists, with the single exception of Prenner, the union manager, were withdrawn at the insistence of Morais.[35] Nonetheless, the opportunity to regain all the demands which Morais had fought for in July had been lost, and the disastrous three-month-old strike finally came to an end.

This first major strike by Jewish workers in the needle trades— a strike previously overlooked by historians of the Jewish labor movement—resulted in a setback for both the anarchists and the union, but it revealed the continuing force of religion in the lives of the Jewish immigrants. The chief participants were Jews of different social, cultural, and religious backgrounds. East European immigrants were pitted against Jews from Germany. The strike, as indeed the earlier labor relations, reflected the divisions within the evolving American Jewish community. The different backgrounds bred distrust and contributed to the bitterness of the strike. Yet, ironically, the common roots of Judaism allowed Rabbi Morais to build upon the Jewish concept of social justice as the basis for arbitration. He bridged the gap between the German Jewish clothiers and the East European Jewish garment workers. He disarmed the anarchists with compassion and thereby gained so much support among the Jewish workers that the anarchists were reluctant to outrage Jewish sensibilities further by irreligious activities such as a projected pork feast at a Yom Kippur ball. The influence of the anarchists declined, just as their tactics had arrested the spontaneous union movement of the immigrant garment workers.[36]

Although the cloakmakers' strike was not the first in the United States to be arbitrated, it was the first in the needle trades and the first in which a rabbi was an arbitrator. Some of the harshness that flared up between employer and striker was softened by Morais' forthright manner. He diffused the influence of the anarchists, and whatever victory the union claimed was the result of his efforts. Rabbinical arbitration, a tradition known to European Jewry, grew out of rabbinic law and practice. It would be employed again later in America when prominent professional men such as Louis D. Brandeis and Louis Marshall sought peaceful solutions to the problems of the garment industry.[37] The conduct of the rabbinate during the strike thus proved to have an enduring effect.

Morais' role had been clear and consistent throughout the

crisis, and was lauded by Jews and non-Jews alike. The *Jewish Exponent* reported favorably on his conduct, although it refrained from discussing the role of the manufacturers. Weeks after the strike had ended, Benjamin Hartogensis of Baltimore wrote to his friend Morais: "It is so very difficult from the conduct of so many rabbis who preach so much and do so little. . . . I rejoice that you have been able to do so much for suffering humanity, that a representative of traditional Judaism was able to show the practical results of his belief in human endeavor despite the protestation of 'liberality' by those who have abjured so many principles of our religion."[38]

Jastrow cooperated with Morais as fully as possible. Only Krauskopf's behavior during the strike appears enigmatic. He attended the meetings during the first weeks of discussion with the manufacturers, but little is known of the views of a man who on other occasions expressed himself ably. For the remainder of the intense period of negotiations, head-clubbing, and rioting, he was absent from the city. It would be unjust to state that Krauskopf was hostile to the strikers or coerced into silence by those of his congregants who were manufacturers, but this may have been true. Despite this, there is no doubt that the strike was a turning point in his career, for in coming years he became involved in many of the civic problems that concerned both non-Jewish Philadelphians and members of the "social justice" movement of the Reform rabbinate: the condition of the Russian immigrants, slum clearance, and improved education.[39]

Morais and Jastrow had done much, but much was left to do. The apparent peace that followed the cloakmakers' strike did not disguise the wretchedness that continued to grip the immigrant community. Throughout the closing decade of the nineteenth century subsequent strikes and protests were effectively suppressed. Technical changes that speeded the production of all ready-made clothing were a boon to the industry, but the degrading conditions which they brought about were not generally known.[40] Immigrant workers were held in contempt, smeared as godless radicals even though they were innocent of the radical currents that were moving into industrial America. After 1892, the influence of the anarchists declined sharply. The two strikes marked the end of a minor episode in American labor history, but it was the beginning of a new epoch in the history of Philadelphia's Jewish labor movement.

## Notes

1. U.S., Congress, House, *Report of the Committee on Manufactures on the Sweating System*, 52nd Cong., 2d sess., 1893, H. Rept. 2309, pp. v–viii.

2. Moses Freeman, *Fifty Years of Jewish Life in Philadelphia* (Philadelphia, 1929), p. 72. [In Yiddish.]

3. Henry S. Morais, *The Jews of Philadelphia* (Philadelphia, 1894), p. 217.

4. Moshe Davis, *The Emergence of Conservative Judaism: The Historical School in Nineteenth Century America* (Philadelphia, 1963), p. 320.

5. *Twenty-eighth Annual Report of the Society of the United Hebrew Charities of Philadelphia* (Philadelphia, 1897), pp. 9–10.

6. Morais, *Jews of Philadelphia*, pp. 217–218.

7. *Proceedings of the Pittsburg Rabbinical Conference: Nov. 16, 17, 18, 1885. Pub. by the Central Conference of American Rabbis in honor of . . . Rabbi Kaufmann Kohler who issued the call for the convention* (Richmond, Va.), pp. 9–10. Emil G. Hirsch, "Elements of Universal Religion," in John H. Barrows, *The World's Parliament of Religions*, 2 (Chicago, 1893), 1306–1307. Joseph Krauskopf, *Glimpses into Judaism* (Philadelphia, Dec. 11, 1887) introduced an unusual series that came to be known as *Sunday Lectures*. They were continued regularly until 1917 and irregularly thereafter.

8. Moshe Davis, "Sabato Morais: A selected and annotated bibliography of his writings . . ." in *Publications of the American Jewish Historical Society*, 37 (1947), 74, 82, 86.

9. *The Jewish Exponent* was founded in 1887 and continues to the present day. It was the successor to *The Jewish Record* pub. from 1875 to 1886. The first newspaper in Yiddish, *Dos Licht* [The Light], was begun in 1891 and lasted ten months.

10. The New York *Yiddishes Tageblatt* [The Yiddish Daily] reached Philadelphia at this time on a regular schedule.

11. Harry Lang and Morris Feinstone, *Gewerkschaften. Jubilee Book Dedicated to 50 Years of Life and Labor of the United Hebrew Trades* (New York, 1938), p. 22. [In Yiddish and English.]

12. Freeman, *Fifty Years of Jewish Life*, pp. 60–66, provides the only

account by contemporaries of the first two attempts at union organization among Jewish garment workers in Philadelphia. Freeman notes that the records of the early unions have vanished.

13. Joseph Cohen, *The Jewish Anarchist Movement in the United States* (Philadelphia, 1945), pp. 96–103, for some of the activities of Pokrass, Prenner, and Staller. [In Yiddish.] *Twentieth Annual Report of the Mount Sinai Hospital* (Philadelphia, 1920), pp. 15–18, for a tribute and an evaluation of Staller's career.

14. Joseph Brandes with Martin Douglas, *Immigrants to Freedom: Jewish Communities in Rural New Jersey since 1882* (Philadelphia, 1971), p. 146; *Who's Who in American Jewry,* 3 (New York, 1938), 65, for members of the Bayuk family.

15. *Who's Who in American Jewry,* 3: 794, for Samuel Paley.

16. *The Press,* Aug. 17, 1891, for a sketch of George Randorf.

17. Freeman, *Fifty Years of Jewish Life,* pp. 61–62, was given this account by Louis Zahn, one of the strikers.

18. *Twenty-First Annual Report . . . United Hebrew Charities* (Philadelphia, 1890), pp. 3 and 44, for Isaac Blum, partner in Blum Brothers, and Gabriel Blum. See also subsequent reports.

19. Freeman, *Fifty Years of Jewish Life,* pp. 74–79, for a view of Jewish anarchists in Philadelphia.

20. Ibid.

21. Ibid., p. 63, for the date of the beginning of the strike.

22. *The Record,* July 20, 1890.

23. See note 14, sup.

24. *Ledger and Transcript,* July 22, 1890.

25. Sermon delivered at Mikveh Israel, Morais Papers, Dropsie University.

26. *Ledger and Transcript,* July 22, 1890.

27. See notes 20 and 22, sup.

28. *Jewish Exponent,* Aug. 8, 1890; *The Record,* Aug. 17, 1890.

29. *Sunday Mercury,* Aug. 10, 1890, contains an interesting account of the reaction of the strikers and their humble surroundings. Freeman, *Fifty Years of Jewish Life,* p. 64; *Jewish Exponent,* Aug. 15, 1890.

30. *Ledger and Transcript,* Aug. 19, 1890, and *The Record,* Aug. 21, 1890, on the employment of Negro women as strikebreakers.

31. *Ledger and Transcript,* Aug. 19, 1890.

32. *Jewish Exponent,* Aug. 15, 1890; *Ledger and Transcript,* Aug. 23, 1890.

33. *Ledger and Transcript,* Aug. 23, 1890.

34. Ibid., Aug. 26, 1890.

35. Ibid.

36. George Randorf to Sabato Morais, Sept. 30, 1890, Morais Papers, advising Morais of the Yom Kippur ball and asking him to intervene.

37. Hyman Berman, "The Cloakmakers' Strike of 1910," in *Essays on Jewish Life and Thought* (New York, 1959), pp. 90–94, for the events leading to the famous "Protocol of Peace" undertaken by laymen rather than rabbis.

38. B. H. Hartogensis to Sabato Morais, Sept. 14, 1890, Morais Papers.

39. Maxwell Whiteman, "Philadelphia's Jewish Neighborhoods," in Allen F. Davis and Mark H. Haller, eds., *The Peoples of Philadelphia* (Philadelphia, 1973), pp. 244–245.

40. *The Record,* Mar. 10, 1894, for a sermon preached by Rabbi Henry Berkowitz of Congregation Rodeph Shalom condemning the sweatshop system.

Chapter 8

# On New Soil
### The Armenian Orthodox and
### Armenian Protestant Churches in the
### New World to 1915

Robert Mirak

Like other immigrants in a strange and distant land, Armenians sought to rebuild their familiar places of worship in America. The immigrants brought with them two religious traditions: the Armenian Orthodox Church and the Armenian Protestant Church. Each functioned in the New World to bridge the gap between the Old and the New, each priest or minister acted as intermediary between the immigrant and the American society, and each church and service reminded the sojourner of home. The Armenian Orthodox Church, especially, linked Armenians to their long and troubled past. It bound Armenians everywhere to the homeland and perpetuated their language, literature, nation, and faith.

As other immigrant groups discovered, the transplanting of the churches involved enormous financial, social, political, and religious decisions. How the two religious traditions fared in the New World, the character of their adjustment, how the churches affected the assimilation of their adherents, and what role they played in an urban environment are the chief concerns of this comparative study of the early history of the Armenian Orthodox and Armenian Protestant Churches in the United States.

The Armenian Orthodox Church, echoing back for centuries, was as old as Rome and the origins of the Armenian nation itself.[1] History and language cut it off from other churches. At the

Council of Chalcedon (451) the Church broke with Byzantium and Rome and was independent thereafter, as it remains to this day.[2] Just before (406) its clerics had invented a separate alphabet for the Armenian language and then had translated the Bible, liturgy, and literature into the Armenian.[3] These events sealed church and nation together. Politically, the Church had exercised a great continuum of power. This was true not only of the medieval period, when the clergy, not the kings, more often dealt with foreign powers and led the nation, but also after the Turkish conquest of the fifteenth century, when Ottoman rule fused its Armenian subjects into a virtual church-state, a condition which endured for four hundred years.[4]

Over the centuries of blighting Turkish rule, the Orthodox Church grew weak, corrupt, and uneducated. A series of attacks on the debilitated Church by Catholic missionaries in the eighteenth century, a far-flung Protestant mission to the Armenians after 1831, and a vibrant, secular, anticlerical movement by the century's close challenged the Church's historic supremacy.[5] Still, the Orthodox Church, however imperfect, prevailed. The transcendant symbol of unity and nation, it acted not only as a vital governing force but also as an asylum and "rallying center," an ark in which "is faithfully preserved all that links him [the Armenian] to the past: traditions, customs, language, literature."[6] The Armenians' violent dispersions and martyrdom sealed the nation to the Church and made the two appear identical.

The Armenian Protestant Church first appeared in the early nineteenth century as the outgrowth of American missionary activity in Turkey. The missionaries' intention had been to proselytize among the Muslim Turks. However, they soon discovered the perils of such an endeavor, and instead sought to "convert" the Orthodox Armenians to the tenets of "true Christianity." This meant, in the view of their organization, the Congregationalist American Board of Commissioners for Foreign Missions, returning the Armenians to the spirit and teachings of the Bible, a repudiation of the ceremonialism of the Orthodox Church, and an emphasis on a well-educated teaching ministry. Their efforts to remain within the fold of the Mother Church were rendered impossible by their own vigorous attacks on the Church and the adamant opposition of the Orthodox hierarchy to the

American mission. By mid-century the missionaries had broken with the Orthodox Church.[7]

After 1860 missionaries actively pursued the growth of a native Protestant Armenian church in Turkey through the establishment of theological schools for native preachers, the widespread dissemination of the Bible in the Armenian vernacular, the establishment of churches and missions in every major city, town, and village in Turkey and the provision of financial support to such institutions. Printing presses, schools, libraries, colleges, and hospitals were also founded.[8]

Converts to the new sect, however, were surprisingly few. According to the American Board, in 1914 there were 137 Protestant churches in Turkey with 50,900 adherents,[9] or about 3 percent of the total Turkish Armenian population. Nonetheless, Armenian Protestantism in Turkey acted as a leaven among Protestants and Orthodox. In stirring educational, social, and religious reform, it taught adherents the goals of "self support," it inculcated an abiding ethicalism, and it withstood the prejudice and persecution of the Orthodox. Its most pervasive influence was in stimulating immigration to the United States.

By 1914 over 65,000 Armenians had fled their homes in the Ottoman Empire and Russia for the New World.[10] The Protestant Armenian Church and especially the American missionaries were particularly important in this movement.

A handful of Armenians had arrived in the New World prior to the nineteenth century, but it was only with the arrival of the Protestant missionaries in 1831 that the first systematic movement of Armenians began to America. Missionaries aroused Armenians' curiosity about America.[11] The first Armenian immigrant in the nineteenth century, Hachadoor Vosganian, arrived in Jacksonian America (1834) as a former missionary student from Constantinople.[12] In time, other students and business people with contacts with Protestants left for America. Powerful disruptive forces after 1890—the massacres of the mid-1890s, 1904, and 1909, the Turkish military draft of Christians after 1910, the desire for economic and religious freedom, and the flight from poverty and oppression—sharply increased the flow.[13] Nonetheless, the exodus to America was a product of American Protestants; without them, immigrants and refugees would have flowed more exclusively to Western Europe, Russia, and Egypt.

Because of the missionaries, Protestants were far more likely than Orthodox Armenians to migrate to America. The number of Protestant Armenians was disproportionately large in the migration. That is, Protestant Armenians in Turkey comprised perhaps 3 percent of the population. Yet upwards of 20 percent of the Armenian immigrants were Protestants.[14] And these immigrants were better educated than the Orthodox because of the large numbers of missionary-educated students and teachers in the migration.[15] All in all, the movement to America owed much of its character to the Protestant missionaries, and the Armenian Protestants were a large factor in the exodus.

Immigrant Armenians concentrated chiefly in the Eastern industrial, urban centers of Massachusetts, Rhode Island, New York, New Jersey, and Pennsylvania, and in a farming outpost in Fresno, California. There, both Armenian Orthodox and Protestant congregations began to establish houses of worship.[16]

The honor of the first Armenian Orthodox Church in America went to Worcester, Massachusetts, in 1891. In Worcester, the first large Armenian-American colony, immigrants took jobs in the wire mills and machine shops as laborers and semi-skilled operatives. The Orthodox immigrants, whose services had been ridiculed by Protestant Armenians in Worcester and who had been termed "scabs" and "Turks" by the local population, looked for a church leader as their spokesman in the alien surroundings. The impetus for a church came from the arrival in 1889 of two powerful Armenian leaders and educators, Mgerdich Portukalian and Michael Tophanelian, who urged the Armenians to found a church and Sunday school to keep their faith and their identity as Armenians. Soon after, the newly founded Armenian Club, which held religious services on Sunday evenings, requested from the Armenian Patriarch in Constantinople an English- or French-speaking priest who was familiar with the New World.[17] The arrival in July 1889 of Father Joseph Sarajian signaled the beginning of regular Orthodox religious services in the New World. The first Armenian Mass, celebrated by Father Sarajian in Worcester that July, was long remembered as a historic occasion by the Worcester immigrants.[18]

Moves for a church building soon followed the church trustees' resolve: "Whereas the Armenian people, by reason of persecution and abject poverty, are immigrating to America, in order to preserve these immigrants from being alienated, we hereby decide to build a church."[19] The church, Surp Prgich (Church of Our Saviour), was founded in accordance with the centuries' long function of the Church: to preserve the Armenians' identity, prevent their assimilation, and keep them as faithful Armenians. A concerted fund-raising drive among Armenians in other East Coast cities and abroad, as well as the hard-earned dollars of the Worcester laboring population, resulted in 1891 in the building of a small but handsome wooden structure on Laurel Hill, in the heart of Worcester's Armenian Quarter.[20]

After 1891, groups formed in Boston, Providence, New York City, Lawrence, and Fresno. In most cases the procedure followed Worcester's. The first step was the formation of a board of trustees *(hokapardzutiun),* usually organized by a prominent Armenian and by the priest. Once assembled, this board canvassed the community for donations to start worship services and form a church. Until a church was built—a step which often consumed many decades of struggle—the board of trustees made arrangements for use of facilities, often with Episcopal churches, with which they felt a kinship.[21] The upstairs room in the New Britain, Connecticut, Church of Christ to this day is called the "Armenian Chapel."[22] Others rented halls. Services were conducted by educated laymen or visiting priests.[23] By the era of World War I (1916), the rapidly growing Armenian-American community had established ten churches with a priesthood of one archbishop and seventeen pastors.[24]

In the same period the Armenian Protestant community built its own New World churches. The Armenian Protestants represented only from 15 to 20 percent of the Armenian-American community. By 1914, however, they had built as many churches as the Orthodox.

As with the Orthodox, the first Protestant Armenian church in the East was built in Worcester. The earliest services by the Armenian Protestant community took place in 1881 in the immigrant lodgings of an Armenian theology student. With increasing immigration, Sunday prayer meetings were held in the Congregationalist church. In the next years, when the Armenian Orthodox established their own church in the city, the small Protestant group sought assistance from the local Protestant Missionary

Association. The American Protestants, some of whom had been missionaries in Turkey, became the critical link in building this religious community and church.[25]

In 1891, for example, American missionaries were holding three Armenian-language services each Sunday in Worcester. They used Bibles and question books written in Armenian and obtained help in singing from American "ladies of the other churches." A moving force of the early Worcester community was the Reverend Albert Hitchcock, a missionary in Turkey who, well versed in the Armenians' language and history, had himself written an Armenian prayer book.[26] Throughout the 1890s the Worcester Missionary Society contributed to the local church group's expenses, including the pastors' entire salaries.[27]

The same assistance was apparent in building the church structure. In 1900 the Armenian Protestant community in Worcester tried to raise a staggering $9,000 for its first Protestant church in Worcester. The meager seventy-member congregation's dramatic efforts raised $1,500 from dollar-by-dollar donations and solicitations. The local Protestants, impressed by the "heroic sacrifices" of the small band of immigrants, thereby donated $6,000 (on the condition of a further Armenian contribution of $1,500)[28] so that on July 14, 1901, the Worcester Armenian Protestant community, which had wandered for twenty years from homes to church halls for worship, joyfully celebrated the cornerstone laying of its Armenian Evangelical Martyrs Church on Pink Street, Worcester.[29]

Soon other churches were purchased or built in West Hoboken, Boston, Lawrence, Lowell, Providence, Philadelphia, Troy, and New York City in the East, and in Fresno, Fowler, Parlier, Yettem, and Los Angeles, California.[30] Most churches were assisted by home missionary associations, as in Worcester, in which cases the Armenians adopted the Congregationalist affiliation. However, where the local Congregationalist community discouraged the Armenians (Troy, 1906), they became Presbyterians.[31] (The only other case of an Armenian Presbyterian church was in Fresno.)

By 1914 the Armenian Protestant community had witnessed a miracle of religious rebirth in the New World. This had been nurtured by their dedication and the efforts of American missionaries and missionary associations. The Protestants' churches had been a great part of their Old World lives; in America they felt out of place praying in an *odar* (non-Armenian, stranger's) church.[32] Accordingly, they insisted on worshiping in their own. The repeated sacrifices of both religious communities testified to the importance they ascribed to maintaining their religious cultures in the New World.

By World War I, the Orthodox community supported churches in the larger East Coast and West Coast communities (with the glaring exception of Boston, whose church was not established until 1923). The immigrants' financial sacrifices in building their churches reflected their deep commitment to the ancient faith. Only within those walls of brick or wood, with priests and services, would they and their families remain Armenians. But, after building the edifices, many found little solace or comfort. For the Church to 1915 was beset by such inner turmoil and problems that it failed to fulfill its mission of assisting immigrants and preserving their heritage in the New World. Long distances from the Old World and the difficulties of communication, a poorly prepared clergy, the Church's abiding traditionalism, and, above all, its recurrent political crises alienated followers from the Mother Church. At the depths of its worst crisis in 1912, a knowledgeable Orthodox observer lamented the Church's condition:

The Armenian Church . . . our chief representative and trustee . . . is a feeble, breathless creature. . . . The great majority of the Armenians in America are not in communication with its influence. . . . I know of many who scoff, for whom religion means ignorance, retrogression, and melancholy. . . . But where are the believers? . . . In Boston of 2500 Gregorian Armenians barely 25 have paid their $2 annual dues. . . . Our pews remain empty, except for Easter and Christmas, and [many are nominal Christians]. The Church is leaderless.[33]

The Church survived the calamities of 1912, but the bitter indictments of historian Vahan Kurkjian were not ill placed.

First of all was the fact of the immigrants' dispersion throughout the United States. According to the Federal Census of 1910, Armenian immigrants were recorded in twenty-five states; by 1910 only three churches, with a dozen priests, were established in the New World.[34] Many widely scattered communities were fortunate even to have a visiting priest offer Holy Communion and solemnize births, marriages, and deaths once a year. Small colonies like Chicago's, which in 1909 had had no religious services for nearly five years, turned out en masse on Sunday to attend a two-and-a-half hour *badarak* (mass) conducted by Father Boghos Kaftanian of Worcester. (Amidst the confusion, crying of children, laughter, and numerous baptisms, the community of immigrants "seemed to have found a long lost thing.")[35]

If communicants were scattered, communications with the Old World were fitful. Until 1898 the New World churches fell under the jurisdiction of the Patriarchate in Constantinople but the jurisdiction was then transferred to Etchmiadzin in Russian Armenia because of the 1894–1896 massacres.[36] The Russian Armenians' terrible trials during the tsarist seizure of Armenian church properties in 1903, the Russian Revolution of 1905, and the turmoil of the ensuing Armeno-Tatar War repeated the earlier disruptions in communications. America was elevated to a missionary diocese in 1898. Yet, bishops often arrived months after their election; in May 1907, for example, the American diocese elected Father Yesnig Abahuni as the new American prelate, but Abahuni did not arrive in the United States until August 1908, fifteen months later.[37]

Nor was the clergy always of high caliber. Perhaps the Patriarchate and the Holy See in Etchmiadzin neglected the New World diocese, but generally priests and bishops were elderly and out of touch with the demands of New World congregations. The Bishop Abahuni, noted above, was aged and in poor health; his critics called him "nervous, tottering, with failing eyesight and accustomed to comfortable living."[38] Another priest in California was implicated in the abduction of a fourteen-year-old Armenian girl in Fresno and, accordingly, disgraced the Armenian community in the local English-language press.[39] Generally, stated one archbishop, rather coldly, the Armenian priests "have been rather ignorant and inefficient and unable to do much for the people in the way of uplift. They do not speak English and hardly know their own tongue. Some speak Turkish."[40] Another critic charged that the priests "come here at an advanced age and never seem to grasp the changes that have taken place in the temper, outlook, and demands of the Armenian immigrants, and so adapt themselves and the churches to meet these changes."[41] Throughout, the needs of the American-born Armenian youth were neglected. To be sure, many humble priests like Father Aharon Melkonian in Fresno (1894–1911) were visible saints laboring endless hours in their parishes for the sick, indigent, and homeless refugees and immigrants. In the aggregate, however, the priests left much to be desired.[42]

Certainly more disruptive to the Church's mission were the recurrent political battles in the newly established parishes. From its inception in the United States in the early 1890s to 1915, the Orthodox Church, the most powerful institution among the Armenians, became the object of personal and political feuds which eroded its power, prestige, and patronage. The politicization of the Church (and community) deeply undermined the mission of the ancient faith.

The background of these battles—the Treaty of Berlin (1878) and the rise of Armenian political parties in the Old World and their endeavors to enlist the immigrants' support for their nationalist-revolutionary causes in Turkey and Russia—is a well-known story.[43] Each party established a New World branch of the turbulent movement active in Turkey and Eastern Europe since the 1890s. The struggles of these parties, the Social Democratic Hnchagian Party ("Hnchags"), the Armenian Revolutionary Federation ("Tashnags"), and the Armenian Constitutional Democratic Party ("Ramgavars") and others repeatedly embroiled the fledgling parishes.[44]

Two notorious episodes—the first in Worcester in 1892–1893, the second two decades later spanning many communities—dramatize the period.

In 1892 the Worcester Armenian community was flooded with Armenian revolutionary propaganda from the Old World preaching immediate armed resistance to the Turkish oppressors. Immediately, the Church, probably under orders from Constantinople, which feared Turkish reprisals, banned the inflammatory literature in Worcester.[45] All hell broke loose. Large numbers of Orthodox members withdrew from the Church and Armenian Club and on the night of March 26, 1893, at the Club, revolutionary sympathizers clashed with Father Sarajian and his group. "Chairs were picked up and a brutal fight followed." The embittered Armenians, "with blood running down their faces, were swinging chair legs through the air." Not only were the Worcester police called to quell the riot and ten persons injured, but the fracas received banner headlines in the *Worcester Daily Telegram,* further disgracing the Armenians.[46] Sarajian eventually resigned in disfavor, but his successor—also an antirevolutionary—similarly irritated the congregation.[47] And a writer bitterly complained that church services at Surp Prgich had not been held for two-and-a-half months because of fear of fighting in the parish.[48] The Church, both willing and unwilling tool of the parties, was hobbled from its mission to the immigrants.

The second crisis began in 1910 and lasted until 1912. The two major parties at that time in the United States, the Tashnags and the Ramgavars, were clashing openly. Partisans of each faction found seats on local church boards of trustees. The path of wisdom among the Church hierarchy was to neutralize the factionalism in the separate churches, maintain order, and thereby minister to the religious and social needs of the immigrants. In 1910, however, the Church, as never before, became totally immersed in the political struggle.

Briefly, the Armenian-American Church assembly elected an avowedly Ramgavar candidate to the prelacy.[49] The election, which was illegally conducted, prompted widespread hostilities. In Chicago (April 1911) opposition to the new prelate led to fistfights and the prelate's flight through a back door. The board of trustees in Boston (July 1911) disputed bitterly whether to permit the newly elected Church head to preach in their pulpit. In Worcester, rival factions battled over his election (October 1911), and in West Hoboken (February 1912) the prelate, forewarned of trouble, relied upon the West Hoboken police force, in attendance at the Holy Mass, to avoid violence.[50] Not for two years, until the prelate, under pressure from his superiors in the Old World, finally left his post, was it possible to restore sorely needed order in the diocese.

These episodes were the most disgraceful and notorious in the colony's early history; however, they were not isolated. Repeatedly, personal and political feuds caused animosity and friction between the boards of trustees, priests, and church assemblies. Turnover among priests was ridiculously high; parish battles were all too common.[51] Certainly the mission of the "once heralded first Christian nation in the world, the martyr church," was diverted from its immigrant parishioners' most important social and personal concerns.

By contrast to 1915, the Armenian Protestant community experienced far fewer difficulties in transplanting to a new soil. The Protestants lacked the Orthodox Church's profound political involvement and its enormous problems of communication with the Old World. Each Protestant church was autonomous. Also, the Protestant clergy were well educated. Accordingly, the Protestant community more successfully fulfilled its New World mission.

To be sure, there were troubling problems. One humiliating experience early faced Armenians in Fresno, California. In 1883 or 1884 the newly arrived Armenian Protestants were asked to combine with native Fresno Congregationalists to establish a first church in the frontier farming community. The Armenians, who had arrived "poor and friendless," had found "good friends," said an Armenian leader, and "our industry has bettered our condition." The combined communities completed their edifice in 1887, after which Armenian families journeyed on horseback, by wagon, or on foot to the First Congregationalist Church for separate Armenian-language services or joined the English-speaking natives in the Sunday morning services. "We were all happy in the kindness exhibited towards us," recalled one Armenian. The harmonious union, however, soon succumbed to prejudice and bigotry. As the number of "Americans" grew in the congregation and the balance of power shifted, the Armenians were no longer welcome. Specifically, a "system of discrimination and persecution against the Armenians" was initiated. The newcomers were ordered to sit by themselves in the church; all hymnbooks and Bibles were removed from their pews; no new Armenians were permitted membership in the church; and finally, their names were stricken from the church membership rolls. All this, in the church which they were invited to help build and support.[52]

The ousted Armenians, who blamed their old clothes, their meager financial support, and even perhaps their garlic eating,

were publicly defended by the Fresno police chief and in the
columns of the *Fresno Daily Republican*. Editorials in their
defense in national religious journals such as the *Boston Congregationalist* and the New York *Outlook* made the situation a
*cause célèbre*—to no avail. Instead, the outcast Armenian
Protestants of Fresno undertook fund raising anew and by 1900
consecrated their second church. This time, however, it was an
Armenian *Presbyterian* church.[53]

Politics, too, occasionally troubled the early parishes.[54] Other
congregations encountered ideological, social, and especially financial problems in this period. On the whole, however, the Armenian Protestant community was spared the debilitating inner
turmoil of the Orthodox community and accordingly enjoyed the
opportunity to carry out its mission in the name of Christ and its
parishioners' needs in a new land. Sympathy for the Armenians
and assistance from missionary groups offset hostility encountered in Fresno.

Such were the inner histories and difficulties of the Orthodox
and Protestant churches in the United States to 1915. And each
influenced the resultant religious culture. Specifically, however,
the effects of these early years on the immigrant churches, the
degree to which the churches resisted the inroads of the New
World's secularizing culture, and the ways they preserved or altered traditions, sharply and markedly varied.

With respect to the Orthodox Church, the most conspicuous
religious change was that much of the religious culture of the Old
World was not transmitted to the New. This was reflected not
only in the dimunition in the numbers of faithful parishioners but
also in the failure of immigrants to observe the rich cycle of religious festivals, holidays, and practices. Of course, it was to be
fully expected in view of the scattering of the Armenians in
America, the competition of other ethnic organizations such as
clubs and political groups, the savage political problems, the
weaknesses of the priesthood, and, more generally, the secularizing nature of a modern industrial urban society.

To be sure, some practices did not change. Certainly the great
religious festivals of Christmas and Easter did not lose their appeal.[55] Yearly, especially at Easter, immigrant families crowded
into tiny, incense-laden churches and halls to hear the celebration

of the ancient mass, join countrymen and priests in singing the *Hayr-Mer* (Our Father) and chanting the *Der Voghormea* (Lord Have Mercy), take communion of the *mas* (unleavened bread) and wine, and listen to a sermon on the Resurrection. After the service the churches' front steps were crowded with men in black derbies and starched collars, women in long black dresses, and multitudes of children all exchanging greetings and conversation. In the church basement or hall immigrants took part in the hallowed practice of cracking the symbollically red or henna colored eggs (dyed in onion skins).

Moreover, the ritual observance of the two-and-a-half hour mass, celebrated every Sunday, remained unchanged as the central rite of the Armenian Orthodox Church. To this day the only important alteration in this ancient mass is the increasing use of the English in the sermon.

Churches also added to the long calendar of days of penance and mourning in the United States by the adoption after 1894 of a day of grieving for the "Dead of Sasun" (site of the 1894 massacres); the holocaust of World War I was thereafter commemorated on April 24, the anniversary of the edict of the Turkish government instituting the deportations and massacres of 1915, which resulted in the annihilation of over 1,000,000 Armenians during the war.[56]

On the other hand, much of the Old World religious practice lapsed. The long calendar of saints' days was no longer observed in its entirety.[57] More critical, the strictures for fasting were not maintained in the New World except by older people, especially women. The Armenian calendar enjoined 160 days of abstinence when only vegetable foods were permitted. In the old country women prepared the vegetables and dried fruits; in America, however, where the strenuous work of the immigrant laborer required a hearty diet, the young men without families ignored the injunctions to abstinence.[58]

More important, the daily matins and vespers and the worship of the average Armenian on a day-to-day basis for five or ten minutes, the practice of kissing the walls of the church or, at least, crossing oneself on passing the sacred building—all this lapsed in busy, industrial America. Certainly most crucial, Sunday church attendance declined everywhere.[59]

Clearly the old religious culture weakened and in some aspects disappeared entirely. However, much more would have been lost had it not been for the handful of dedicated priests, boards of trustees, and the hitherto neglected immigrant women. For it was the Armenian women who staunchly supported the Church and its ancillary institutions which sought to preserve the old ways. Specifically, the Sunday schools and Armenian language schools, though supervised by the local priest, in fact were the sole responsibility of the female parishioners, who staffed them, prepared their materials, and furnished the budget.[60] Women also supported church-based charities.[61] The Church owed much to the dedicated women who worked ceaselessly amid all the turmoil for the preservation of the religious life and the preservation of Armenian culture in America.

The old religious culture of the Orthodox slowly lapsed in America for a variety of complex reasons. Its basic mission—the preservation of the old culture in the New World—was undermined. By contrast, the Armenian Protestant Church acted as a willing acculturating mechanism in the New World. The Protestants did not lay stress on the old language and culture. Rather, they preached the new religion of Congregationalism, which promoted the adoption of New World and American ways. The Armenian Protestant Church was a willing halfway house between the old religious culture and modern, twentieth-century American Congregationalism.

To be sure, Armenian Protestant ministers (*badvellis*) gave resolute affirmation to their Armenian patriotism. "We are not to grow just as a 'church' or any church, but grow as an *Armenian* Church," testified the Reverend A. A. Bedikian, a saintly and generous leader of the Armenian Protestant Church. "The *raison d'être* of an Armenian Church is being *Armenian*," he further concluded.[62] And, as an example of their patriotism, the Old World language was exclusively used in the early services. In fact, there were also allowances for the Turkish-speaking members of the congregation who came from Adana or Marash. The Second Armenian Congregational Church of Philadelphia had the unusual distinction of a regular bilingual service: the *badvelli* delivered a sermon in Armenian, then one in Turkish, on different topics, since some of his parishioners knew both languages.

Hymns from Elmassian's bilingual hymnal were sung in Armenian and Turkish simultaneously which made it sound, said one young Armenian Protestant, like a Tower of Babel.[63] In any case, Armenian was an integral part of the earliest Protestant services.

In time, however, English supplanted Armenian in the churches, especially for the younger generation, who were insufficiently versed in Armenian to follow services in that language.[64] William Saroyan recalled that in Fresno in the 1920s the entire service, except for the sermon, was given in English.[65] In the 1930s, the Philadelphia congregation, which used Turkish and Armenian, added English for trilingual services for some years.[66] Increasingly, English made inroads in the Protestant churches.

In this connection it appears that the *badvellis,* unlike the Orthodox priests, rarely urged their parishioners to speak the ancestral language at home. Whereas in an Orthodox parish many sermons each year were devoted to encouraging use of the language, especially among the young, this was not true in Protestant congregations.[67] Indeed, nationalistic Armenians berated the Protestants for permitting the language to lapse and quoted one *badvelli* as saying: "For me, there is no Armenia, only America. We left Armenian things in Turkish-Armenia; here we must be Americans. I am an American and I teach my children no Armenian." Religious themes rather than nationalistic injunctions or stories about Armenian history formed the core of the Protestant Armenians' sermons.[68]

More pragmatically and importantly, the *badvellis*—English-speaking, American-educated, and knowledgeable—were of inestimable assistance in acculturating the bewildered and helpless immigrants to the demands of urban America. Again, by contrast with the Orthodox priests, who encountered adjustment problems of their own, the Armenian *badvellis* aided newcomers through a host of ways: writing letters in English, making bank deposits, purchasing land or property, and dealing with immigration authorities, the courts, or the law. Armenians seeking work were placed in jobs. The well-educated and well-spoken Armenian Protestant ministers also helped immigrants cleanse their reputations as strike-breakers, "goddamned Armenians," and "goddamned Turks."[69]

Indeed, by 1901, much Protestant effort went into immigrant

assistance through the Armenian Colonial Association, which maintained offices in Marseilles, New York, and Chicago to aid newcomers. The ACA was of incalculable assistance to the immigrants at the major stopping port of Marseilles, and at Ellis Island in providing funds, advice, and ultimately jobs. Informally, the fact that the *badvellis* also had close personal ties with prominent American missionaries and churchmen was an additional vital resource for immigrants in urban America.[70]

In addition, Armenian ministers adopted such American innovations as Sunday schools and Christian Endeavor societies to fuse evangelical Christianity and social ethics. These and the young men's and young women's lyceums, meeting once or twice weekly, were often devoted to informing immigrants about life in the American city and gave talks on such topics as the proper diet for the city family, life in the tenement, child care, and the necessity of exercise in the city.[71]

From the pulpits the *badvellis* also acculturated their congregations with the ethical core of modern American Congregationalism, and the temptations of the new urban environment were not neglected. Emphases were laid on ethicalism, biblical literalism, and abstinence. Indeed, abstinence from drink was an eleventh commandment. Thus *badvellis* severely rebuked Armenian picnic-goers who drank beer or *raki* (oghi); Armenian coffeehouses were termed not places of relaxation, but of dissipation. Drinking, smoking, gambling, and modern "breast to breast" dancing were all condemned.[72] One secular critic in California excoriated both Protestant and Orthodox clerics for neglecting the rampant evils of the tenderloin and the Chinese gambling houses in Fresno patronized by young immigrants.[73] But the *badvellis* generally administered a heavy dose of fundamentalist American moralism. Indeed, the injunctions against such activities were so strong that one son of an Armenian minister remembered the feeling that "anything that brought supreme pleasure was wrong."[74]

The core of the *badvellis'* message emphasized modern American Protestant religious dogma and social ethics. However, it would be an error to equate the immigrant Protestant churches with the modern, wealthy American Congregationalist or Presbyterian churches of the period. Most were small and poverty-

stricken, and not a few members of the younger generation, of-
fended by the "immigrant" or "old country" status of the
churches, sought religious consolation in "American" churches.
Thus one girl wrote of the Protestant church services in a rented
hall in Boston:

[The room] was sparse and wretched. . . . There were sparse old
wooden chairs on a dirty wooden floor, . . . a huge square old piano
with thick legs and feet. . . . The pulpit was nothing more than a small
wooden platform with an oak bookstand. On it sits a Bible with a worn
out cover. . . . There are hymnals without covers scattered here and
there. [As for the atmosphere of the place] there is the smell of smoke
and onions. . . . There is confusion—women bring their children who
play or quarrel . . . while the infants are being suckled. . . . The
*badvelli* starts the service . . . assisted by a boy at the piano . . . and
the congregation, out of tune, joins them.[75]

The odious and distasteful stigma of the immigrant church was so
strong that one second-generation *badvelli* who was called to the
pastorate of an Armenian Protestant church in New England
insisted that the "new" church discard all old furniture, hand-me-
down lamps, second-hand pianos, rugs, and dilapidated furnish-
ings which recalled the old immigrant days of rented halls and
poverty. The jump from the Old World to respectability took
more than one generation.[76]

On balance, the Protestant churches did willingly and force-
fully represent an important mediating step between the Old
World and the New. Their parishioners more quickly learned
English, adopted new ways, made their life in the United States,
and became "Americanized." Unquestionably, with respect to
the role of the Armenian churches in the New World, the
paramount and undeniable difference between the two churches
lay in the area of acculturation. One—the Orthodox—stood,
staunchly and resolutely, for the preservation in toto of the Old;
this was its historic justification, its rationale, and a source of its
weakness. It was also its glory. On the other hand, there was the
smaller, equally poor, but more modernizing Armenian Protestant Church, which stood halfway between the Old and the New.

Such is the outline to World War I of the story of two religious
cultures, exiled from their "ruined nests" in Turkey and Russia,
and how they came to terms with the challenges and high promise
of the New World.

## Notes

1. The Armenian Orthodox Church is also referred to as the Armenian Apostolic Church because of the tradition of its founding by the apostles Thaddeus and Bartholomew, and the Armenian Gregorian Church after St. Gregory, who was responsible for the conversion of the Armenians to Christianity in the early fourth century.

The dating of the conversion of Armenia to Christianity is controversial. The long-accepted date is 301; however, recent scholarship is more inclined to set it at 314. The most reliable general history of the Armenian Orthodox Church in English is Malachia Ormanian, *The Church of Armenia*, 2nd ed. (London, 1955). A brief useful account is in Sirarpie Der Nersessian, *The Armenians* (New York, 1970). A good survey of Armenian Christianity is Leon Arpee, *A History of Armenian Christianity* (New York, 1946). Indispensable is Malachia Ormanian's *Azkabadum*, 3 vols. (Constantinople-Jerusalem, 1913–1927).

2. The Armenian Church broke with the great churches of Byzantium and Rome in 451 but remained in communion with the Syriac churches of Antioch and Persia, the Church of Alexandria, the Caucasian Albanians, and the Georgians (until the sixth century). The official schism occurred at the Council of Dvin (506). The most authoritative work on the schism is Karekin Sarkissian, *The Council of Chalcedon and the Armenian Church* (London, 1965).

3. Der Nersessian, *The Armenians*, pp. 84ff.

4. For a brief, useful description of the church-state under the Ottomans see Avedis Sanjian, *The Armenian Communities in Syria under Ottoman Dominion* (Cambridge, Mass., 1965), pp. 31–45. Also, H. A. R. Gibb and Harold Bowen, *Islamic Society and the West*, 2 vols. (Oxford, 1950–1957) 1, pt. 2: 207–261.

5. For the corruption of the Church see Eli Smith, *Researches . . . in Armenia*, 2 vols. (Boston, 1833), 1:58; Leon Arpee, *The Armenian Awakening* (Chicago, 1909), p. 173; and Sanjian, *Armenian Communities in Syria*, p. 35. The story of the Catholic movements in Armenia remains to be told in English. A useful pamphlet issued on the 300th anniversary of the birth of the founder of the order, Abbot Mekhitar, is Kevork Bardakjian, *The Mekhitarists Contributions to Armenian Culture and Scholarship* (Cambridge, Mass., 1976). Citations regarding the Protestant excision are below, notes 7–10. For the revolutionary movement, a useful introduction is Louise Nalbandian, *The Armenian Revolutionary Movement* (Berkeley, 1963), chap. 2.

6. Ormanian, *The Church of Armenia*, p. xiv. The quotation is from the preface by Bertrand Bareilles.

7. For the origins of the movement see *Missionary Herald*, Mar. 1868; *Historical Sketch of the Missions in European Turkey, Asia Minor*

*and Armenia* (New York, 1861); Smith, *Researches . . . in Armenia;* and Arpee, *The Armenian Awakening,* chaps. 6 and 7.

8. Arpee, *History of Armenian Christianity,* pp. 275ff.

9. American Board of Commissioners for Foreign Missions, *Annual Reports, 1914,* p. 107. The statistics are for the year 1913. Also, Ormanian, *Church of Armenia,* p. 209.

10. The most recent account of the migration to the United States to World War I is Robert Mirak, "Armenian Emigration to the United States to 1915 (part I): Leaving the Old Country," *Journal of Armenian Studies,* 1 (Autumn 1975), 5–29. An appendix by the author and Alice K. Mirak, "Armenian Immigration to the United States, 1834–1914: A Statistical Analysis," seeks to quantify the movement. The period from 1914 to the 1930s is covered by Edward Minasian, "The Armenian Immigrant Tide," *Recent Studies in Modern Armenian History* (Cambridge, Mass., 1972), pp. 105–117.

11. Cyrus Hamlin, *Among the Turks* (New York, 1878), chaps. 12 and 14.

12. Mirak, "Armenian Emigration . . . to 1915," p. 8.

13. Ibid., pp. 14–29.

14. No statistics exist for the religious affiliations of the immigrants. One eyewitness in the Ottoman Empire stated, in speaking of the Armenians: "in proportion to their numbers, the Protestants in Turkey have furnished by far the largest number of emigrants" (James L. Barton, *Daybreak in Turkey* [Boston, 1908], p. 236). Estimates of the Armenians in the United States uniformly place the Protestants at 15 to 25 percent of the total. See M. Vartan Malcom, *The Armenians in America* (Boston, 1919), p. 99 for 15 percent, and Eldridge Mix, "Armenians of Worcester," *Worcester Magazine* (1902) for 25 percent.

15. Teachers formed the single largest category of professional people in the migration, or 1 percent of the total. See U.S., Bureau of Immigration, *Annual Reports, 1899–1914,* prepared by Commissioner-General of Immigration. No category existed for students, but American missionaries repeatedly bewailed the flight of "our students" to the United States. See, for example, Bitlis Field Report, 1887, American Board of Commissioners for Foreign Missions, Manuscripts, 16.9.7, Vol. 6, Harvard College Library.

16. The largest concentrations of Armenian immigrants in 1910 were in Massachusetts, New York, California, Rhode Island, New Jersey, Illinois, Pennsylvania, and Connecticut. U.S., Bureau of the Census, *Thirteenth Census 1910,* (Washington, D.C., 1913), 1:982, 1005. The story of the communities to 1915 is in Robert Mirak, "The Armenians in the United States, 1890–1915" (unpub. doctoral dissertation, Harvard University, 1965).

17. The story of the first church in Worcester is in Mushegh Seropian, ed., *Amerigahai Daretsuitse, 1913* (Boston, 1913), pp. 49ff; the Reverend Arten Ashjian, *Vijagatsuits ev Badmutiun Arhachnortagan Themin Hayots Amerigayi* (New York, 1949), pp. 18–20, 277–282. A recent thoroughly researched study is the Reverend Oshagan Minassian, "A History of the Armenian Holy Apostolic Orthodox Church in the United States (1888–1944)" (unpub. doctoral dissertation, Boston University School of Theology, 1974). A brief, useful description is in *Dedication of the Armenian Church of Our Saviour Cultural Center* (Worcester, 1968).

18. *Worcester Daily Telegram*, Aug. 22, 1893.

19. Ashjian, *Vijagatsuits ev Badmutiun*, p. 278. Trans. in *Dedication of the Armenian Church.*

20. Ashjian, *Vijagatsuits ev Badmutiun*, pp. 279–282. Seropian, ed., *Amerigahai Daretsuitse, 1913*, pp. 70ff.

21. U.S., Dept. of Commerce, Bureau of the Census, *Religious Bodies: 1916*, 2:37.

22. Archibald Hovanesian Jr., "The Armenian Community: A Study in Social Change" (unpub. bachelor's thesis, Princeton, 1962), p. 100.

23. Ashjian, *Vijagatsuits ev Badmutiun*, pp. 188–189, for the Philadelphia story.

24. U.S., *Religious Bodies: 1916*, 2:39.

25. Seropian, ed., *Amerigahai Daretsuitse, 1913*, pp. 357ff.

26. *Worcester Daily Telegram*, Jan. 12, 1891.

27. Worcester, *City Missionary Reports, 1893–1897;* Seropian, ed., *Amerigahai Daretsuitse, 1913*, pp. 381ff.

28. Worcester, *City Missionary Reports, 1897; Gotchnag*, July 13, 1901.

29. *Gotchnag*, July 20, 1901.

30. Malcom, *Armenians in America*, p. 100.

31. *Gotchnag*, Mar. 28, 1908; *Hairenik*, May 26, 1906.

32. *Gotchnag*, Jan. 26, 1907.

33. Ibid., Aug. 3, 1912. For other criticisms in the same vein see ibid., Nov. 18, 1911, Aug. 24, 1912, July 26, 1913; *Azk*, Feb. 23, Oct. 26, 1910; *Hairenik*, May 11, 1907.

34. U.S., *Fourteenth Census, 1920* (Washington, D.C., 1923), 2:1008–1009 gives figures for 1910 and 1920. The locations of the three churches were Worcester, Fresno, and West Hoboken. Ashjian, *Vijagatsuits ev Badmutiun*, pp. 23, 278ff.

35. *Azk*, Nov. 10, 1909.

36. Ormanian, *Azkabadum*, 3: 5102–5105.

37. *Hairenik*, June 22, 1907, Oct. 3, 1908; *Azk*, Feb. 29, 1908, for details of his trip to America. Ashjian, *Vijagatsuits ev Badmutiun*, pp. 24–25.

38. *Hairenik*, June 22, 1907.

39. *Hairenik*, July 28, 1906; *Gotchnag*, Aug. 4, 1906; *Fresno Morning Republican*, July 12, 1906.

40. *The People of the Eastern Orthodox Churches; Report of the Commission Appointed by the Missionary Department of New England . . . 1912* (Springfield, Mass., 1913). The comment is by Archbishop Mushegh Seropian.

41. Malcom, *Armenians in America*, p. 103.

42. Mushegh Seropian, ed., *Amerigahai Daretsuitse, 1912* (Boston, 1912), p. 64.

43. Helpful English-language accounts differing in interpretation of the background are Nalbandian, *The Armenian Revolutionary Movement*, and William L. Langer, *The Diplomacy of Imperialism* (New York, 1951), especially chap. 5.

44. The Armenian Constitutional Democratic Party, founded in 1908, became the Armenian Democratic Liberal Party in 1920. It was referred to throughout the period as the Ramgavar Party. The only important study of the political parties in the United States is Manug Jizmejian, *Badmutiun Amerigahai Kaghakagan Gusagtsuteants, 1890–1925* (Fresno, Calif., 1930). It must be used with caution.

45. Ormanian, *Azkabadum*, 3:5102–5105; Jizmejian, *Badmutiun Amerigahai*, pp. 19ff.

46. The *Worcester Daily Telegram*, Mar. 27, 1893, carried the following headlines: "Priest Was in the Fight!"; "Bloody Riot"; and "Armenians Smash Each Other with Tables and Chairs." See also Seropian, ed., *Amerigahai Daretsuitse, 1913*, pp. 86ff.

47. *Worcester Daily Telegram*, Apr. 3, Aug. 22, 1893. Seropian, ed., *Amerigahai Daretsuitse, 1913*, pp. 74ff. Sarajian's successor, Father Magakia Derunian (1894–1897) conceded that his politics "may be antagonistic to those of the majority of Armenians in America," *Worcester Daily Telegram*, Mar. 29, 1894.

48. This was during the period of Father Mashtots Papazian (1897–1898). For his brief, stormy pastorate see Seropian, ed., *Amerigahai Daretsuitse, 1913*, pp. 105ff, and *Yeprad*, Dec. 18, 1897, Jan. 1, Feb. 19, Mar. 12, and Aug. 20, 1898.

49. The center of the storm was Archbishop Mushegh Seropian, who arrived in the United States in late 1910; see *Azk*, Nov. 30, 1910. For his pro-Ramgavar position, see ibid., Feb. 15, 1911. For discussion of his disputed election see *Hairenik*, Mar. 7, 1911, and *Gotchnag*, Apr. 1, 1911. Disputes also surrounded the legality of his being in the United States; see *Gotchnag*, May 18, 1912, and *Asbarez*, May 24, 1912.

50. *Hairenik*, Apr. 4, July 18, Oct. 31, 1911, Feb. 27, 1912.

51. Worcester was ministered to by seven different priests between 1899 and 1912. In the same period there were nine different priests in the Providence parish. Ashjian, *Vijagatsuits ev Badmutiun*, pp. 211 and 288.

52. William Starratt et al., *Astounding Persecution of Armenian Christians in Central California* (n. p., n. d.), contains extracts from contemporaneous newspaper accounts of the episode. See also the Reverend William N. Meserve, *Extracts from a letter of a former pastor of the Fresno Church* (n. p., n. d.). Also, see Seropian, ed., *Amerigahai Daretsuitse, 1912,* pp. 63ff.

53. Seropian, ed., *Amerigahai Daretsuitse, 1913,* pp. 373–374; Ben Randal Walker, *Fresno County Blue Book* (Fresno, Calif., 1941), p. 233. At the same time, a smaller, dissident group of ousted church members split from the newly formed Presbyterian Church to form the Armenian Pilgrims Congregational Church which relied on the use of rented halls until 1907 when it purchased its own building. In 1912, this group purchased the original Congregational Church which had ousted them in 1894 as the native American congregation fled the neighborhood before the waves of newly arrived immigrants. See *Fresno Morning Republican,* Mar. 25, 1907, and Seropian, ed., *Amerigahai Daretsuitse, 1913,* pp. 374ff.

54. The only turbulent political episode occurred in Worcester under the pastorate of the Reverend Karekin Chitjian. For his biography see Vahe Haig, ed., *Kharpert ev ir Vosgetashd* (New York, 1959), pp. 1113ff. The story in Worcester is in Jizmejian, *Badmutiun Amerigahai,* pp. 10–11; Seropian, ed., *Amerigahai Daretsuitse, 1913,* pp. 378–379; *Worcester Daily Telegram,* Jan. 4, 1894.

55. Regarding the dates of Armenian festivals, prior to 1923 the Armenians, like other Eastern churches, used the ancient Julian calendar which, in the twentieth century, was thirteen days behind the new (Gregorian) calendar. In dating the moveable festivals, such as Easter, the Armenians employed the Nicene computation which, identical with the Greek Orthodox Church, seldom synchronized with the Western churches. In 1923 the Church adopted the Gregorian calendar, but to this day the Armenian Church continues to celebrate Christmas in conjunction with the Theophany (Baptism of Christ) on Jan. 6, Ormanian, *Church of Armenia,* chap. 37.

56. The first memorial to the Armenians massacred at Sasun in the summer of 1894 took place on Thanksgiving Day, 1894, in Worcester; *Worcester Daily Telegram,* Nov. 26, 30, 1894. The observation of the Genocide, which commenced on April 24, 1915, is universally commemorated in Armenian communities on that day each year.

57. Interview, the Reverend Papken Maksoudian, Cambridge, Mass., Aug. 18, 1971.

58. Ibid.; Ormanian, *The Church of Armenia,* pp. 155–156.

59. Interview, the Reverend Maksoudian, Aug. 18, 1971; Ormanian, *The Church of Armenia,* p. 154. Complaints about lapses in attendance were everywhere. "The Armenian people have always been warm supporters of religion in general and their venerable church in particular. But

here in the United States they manifest an apparent lack of interest"
(Malcom, *Armenians in America,* p. 102). "Armenians of Worcester,"
*Worcester Magazine,* Aug., 1902: "Many of them [Orthodox] have
thrown off all obedience . . . and are estranged from the church of their
fathers."

60. For the role of the women in each parish see Ashjian, *Vijagatsuits
ev Badmutiun,* pass. For their statistics in the United States see U.S.,
*Religious Bodies: 1916,* 2:40.

61. U.S., *Religious Bodies: 1906,* 2:39.

62. Quoted in Nazareth Barsumian, *Stowaway to Heaven* (Wilmette,
Ill., 1961), p. 194.

63. Interview, the Reverend Vartan Hartunian, Belmont, Mass.,
Aug. 20, 1971. Also, *Gotchnag,* Mar. 1, 1902.

64. See Charles Mahakian, "History of the Armenians in California"
(unpub. master's thesis, University of California, Berkeley), reprinted
by R and E Research Associates, San Francisco, 1974, p. 48. A fascinating and much neglected work on the early community with comments on the use of English in Protestant services is Hagop Kuyumjian,
*Aha Kezi Ameriga* (Boston, 1949), pp. 496–504.

65. William Saroyan, "Sunday is a Hell," *I Used to Believe I Had
Forever, Now I'm Not so Sure* (New York, 1968), p. 18.

66. Interview, the Reverend Hartunian, Aug. 20, 1971.

67. Ibid.

68. *Hairenik,* May 5, 1906.

69. For the caliber of the clergy see comments on the Reverend M. G.
Papazian, *Fresno Morning Republican,* July 13, 1919; the Reverend M.
S. Knadjian, in Saroyan, "First Armenian . . . Church," *Places Where
I've Done Time* (New York, 1972), pp. 170–171; the Reverend A. A.
Bedikian, a "saint" of the Armenian Protestant Church, was a gradu-
ate of Yeprad Theological School (Kharpert) and Yale Divinity School.
See also Malcom, *Armenians in America,* p. 102.

70. Mirak, "Armenians in the United States, 1890–1915," pp. 79–81.

71. Worcester, *City Missionary Society Reports, 1897.*

72. On abstinence see, for example, *Gotchnag,* Mar. 29, 1913. For
criticism of coffeehouses and drinking at picnics see *Gotchnag,* Sept. 1,
1906, July 11, 1908, Feb. 13, 1913; the May 27, 1911 issue spoke out
against "modern dancing."

73. *Asbarez,* Mar. 22, 1912.

74. The recollection is by the Reverend Vartan Hartunian, interview,
Aug. 20, 1971.

75. *Gotchnag,* July 5, 12, 1902.

76. Interview, the Reverend Hartunian, Aug. 20, 1971.

# Contributors

JOSEF J. BARTON (Ph.D. Michigan), Associate Professor of History and of Urban Affairs at Northwestern University, is the author of *Peasants and Strangers* and several articles on immigration. His current research interest is immigration and working-class communities in Chicago.

DENNIS J. CLARK (Ph.D. Temple) has written numerous books and articles on urban affairs, race relations, and immigrant history. A graduate of Saint Joseph's College, he has maintained a close interest in Philadelphia. Currently, he is doing research on immigrant children and Irish fraternal organizations. He is Executive Director of the Samuel S. Fels Fund in Philadelphia.

JAY P. DOLAN (Ph.D. Chicago) is Assistant Professor of History at Notre Dame University and advisory editor for the Arno Press series on the American Catholic Tradition. He has published numerous articles on immigrant and church history as well as one book, *The Immigrant Church*. His new book on American Catholic revivalism will be published shortly.

WILLIAM J. GALUSH (Ph.D. Minnesota) has written several articles on immigrant history and is writing a book on Polish immigrants in America (Indiana University Press). He is Associate Professor of History at Loyola University of Chicago.

161

THOMAS D. MARZIK (Ph.D. Columbia) is Assistant Professor of History at Saint Joseph's College. He has published articles on T. G. Masaryk and is engaged in research on Slovak and Czech national movements in the late nineteenth and early twentieth centuries.

RANDALL M. MILLER (Ph.D. Ohio State) has written numerous articles and one book on eighteenth- and nineteenth-century American life and history, particularly the Southern experience. He is Assistant Professor of History at Saint Joseph's College.

ROBERT MIRAK (Ph.D. Harvard) teaches in the history department at Boston University and manages his own business. He has written several articles on Armenian immigration to the United States.

M. MARK STOLARIK (Ph.D. Minnesota), a native-born Slovak, is the author of one book and several articles on Slovak immigration and ethnic history. Currently, he is Historical Researcher for the Canadian Centre for Folk Culture Studies, National Museums of Canada, Ottawa.

RUDOLPH J. VECOLI (Ph.D. Wisconsin) is Professor of History and Director of the Immigration History Research Center at the University of Minnesota. He has published numerous books and articles on Italian immigration, ethnic, and social history.

MAXWELL WHITEMAN, Archivist and historian at The Union League of Philadelphia, has written numerous books and articles on a wide range of subjects. He is completing a book on the history of East European Jewish immigrants in Philadelphia. He is a Commissioner on the Pennsylvania Historical and Museum Commission and a juror on the Pennsylvania Hall of Fame.

# Index